Psychological Man

Psychological Man

Harry Levinson

The Levinson Institute, Incorporated
Cambridge, Massachusetts

Library of Congress Cataloging in Publication Data

Levinson, Harry.
  Psychological man.

  Includes bibliographical references.
  1. Psychology, Industrial. 2. Psychoanalysis.
I. Title. [DNLM: 1. Personality. 2. Psychology,
Industrial. 3. Psychoanalytic theory. WA495 L657p]
HF5548.8.L384   158.7   76-2583
ISBN 0-916516-01-6
ISBN 0-916516-02-4 pbk.

Fifth Printing

To the memory of Ralph M. Hower
an exemplar of the highest qualities
of a professor:
readiness to learn and willingness to help

Contents

Contents

Illustrations

Preface

In 1953, I was asked by Dr. William C. Menninger to undertake a program of prevention of mental illness among adults. Those were the days before community psychiatry and community psychology. There were few guidelines and almost no direction. I assumed that if one were to undertake prevention among adults that would mean working with the organizations in which they worked because not only do employed adults spend nearly half of their waking time at work, but also their occupational experience is highly relevant to how they feel about themselves and to the stress they experience.

With a grant from the Rockefeller Brothers Fund, I undertook a nose-following expedition of some 60,000 miles around the United States talking to people in personnel work, to industrial psychologists and industrial physicians, industrial psychiatrists, executives, and many others to try to get a grasp on the extent and expression of emotional maladjustment in organizations.

I was appalled to discover that while there were many people in companies and other organizations who were concerned about motivation and many psychologists and others had studied motivational issues, the conceptions of motivation with which industrial psychologists, personnel specialists, executives, and others worked bore no resemblance to the complex understanding of personality which my clinical colleagues required to be able to work therapeutically with people. It was as if there were a body of engineering knowledge on the one hand while on the other there were people busy building bridges who had no awareness that there was such a body of knowledge and experience. Those who had some awareness of that knowledge simply ignored it.

This exploratory experience led to: (1) the evolution of seminars for executives and industrial physicians on the application of psychoanalytic theory to management problems and leadership; (2) field work in organizations to develop a diagnostic and intervention method; (3) consultation with companies, churches, schools, and governmental organizations; (4) involvement in management education through university courses, company and governmental training programs, industry and corporate meetings, public speeches, and a large number of articles and books.

I found it necessary to reconceptualize industrial psychology and sociology in the context of the clinical framework I had already developed. Thus, my work is what might even be called applied clinical sociology. In it, I have tried to interrelate complex personality theory, empirical findings, and organizational conceptions in a way that allows both the executive and the consultant to discern problems and act on them, even if there is not yet the experimental or research support for the directions offered. The internal consistency of the theory makes it possible to work with the same assumptions about personality whether one is dealing with executive stress, management development, selection, compensation, motivation, or organizational design.

The original field work in the Kansas Power and Light Company (*Men, Management and Mental Health*) led to the conception of the psychological contract. Consultation with executives about emotional problems in their organizations and about counselling programs resulted in *Emotional Health: In The World of Work* and *Executive Stress* (Harper & Row), which are systematic treatments of characteristic personality structures and characteristic on-the-job problems, respectively. The need to integrate the several fields gave rise to *The Exceptional Executive* (Harvard University Press) which is the only integration of all of the major managerial psychology theories into a single systematic conception of the contemporary leadership task. Consultation with organizations made clear, the need for *Organizational Diagnosis* (Harvard University Press), a comprehensive, systematic outline for gathering data on the multiple facets of an organization for purposes of organizing and distilling these data into a diagnostic statement as a basis for organizational change. The underlying assumption is that diagnosis is a running hypothesis which is always subject to being tested and corrected. All consultation is based on diagnosis, which, however, usually is not made explicit. In addition, one must separate fact from inference from interpretation before acting either as an executive or a consultant.

In 1968 I went to the Harvard Graduate School of Business Administration as Thomas Henry Carroll-Ford Foundation Distinguished Visiting Professor. The papers of the next four years became *The Great Jackass Fallacy* (Harvard University Press). These papers cover a range of topics, using the same conceptions of motivation to illustrate the applicability of the concepts to a wide array of managerial problems, issues, and functions. In that book I point out the limits of reward-punishment psychology and contemporary nonclinical versions of motivation. This is not to say that these orientations are of no value; rather, it is to say that without a *comprehensive theory of personality* they are severely limited.

Psychological Man represents a consolidation and expansion of everything I have written before. It is essentially an introduction to the theory with which I work, integrating the work of many others, and an outline of how that theory may be applied to understanding executive stress, management by objectives, performance appraisal, supervision, leadership, compensation, selection and placement, organizational structure, and the age- and stage-specific psychological tasks and problems of people at work. It is intended for managers and executives who are interested in becoming acquainted with this dimension of management; for people in personnel, training, and organizational development, who want to develop a solid, systematic base in personality theory for what they do; for MBA students and others who are dissatisfied with the limitations of the generalities about motivation.

The first part of this book is my statement of the theory, followed by implications and applications. That way, though most people abjure theory, the reader will know where I am coming from and the logic upon which I base my statements. Besides, I think management psychology should approach the level of the rest of psychology and recognize complexity in the same way that engineering, accounting, finance, and other disciplines do. The field has been simplistic for too long.

The reader who will want greater depth may follow up by pursuing one or another of the books from which much of this material is drawn. Some chapters like "Management By Guilt" in *Emotional Health*, and "A Psychologist Diagnoses Merger Failures," "Conflicts That Plague Family Businesses," and "On The Experience Of Personal Loss" in *The Great Jackass Fallacy* are, to my knowledge, the only pieces on these topics in the management literature.

In essence, coming from a clinical orientation into the management psychology area, I have had to teach myself. My writings are my primary method for integrating what I learn into a guide for myself and others. This summary is intended to serve that guiding and bridging function for the reader.

The title derives from chapter two of *The Great Jackass Fallacy*. In that book I delineated four major conceptions or models of man. The first was the traditional conception of economic man, motivated by the quest for money. The second was social man, motivated by the need for relationships with his fellows. This view is exemplified by the humanistic movement, which grew out of the Hawthorne studies and those who follow that tradition. The third, self-actualizing man, derived from a work of Maslow on which much of contemporary organizational behavior and industrial psychology is based. Finally comes psychological man, a conception which includes a comprehensive understanding of a configuration or complex set of interacting forces both within the person and between the person and his environment, which results in behavior. This book describes and defines what I mean by psychological man in greater detail.

A word about the contents. Most articles and books in the field of industrial psychology and organization development are built around general topics. These are largely empirical works with limited conceptualization. Every psychologist and sociologist or organizational development specialist has implicitly in mind some model of man as he writes. Very few people specify their model, and they are therefore hard put to derive the theories and recommendations they make from an explicit statement of personality. This fact has resulted in the jumble of odds and ends which comprises most of this field. I have therefore very clearly stated the model of man with which I work in the first chapter. In the second chapter I have pointed out the implications of this model for the points of psychological vulnerability and psychological stress that most people are likely to experience. In the third chapter I have extended and extrapolated from the theory to logical conclusions about selection, assignment, appraisal, compensation, organizational change, and similar issues. In that chapter I have also tried to integrate the work of numerous others. In the final chapter I have indicated what I think some of the future issues and problems are likely to be in this field and therefore the relevance of this book. By so doing, I am inviting the reader to look at the psychological assumptions behind the applications that I suggest and recommend. That way I hope to call the reader's attention to the importance of assumptions about personality as well as to encourage others to specify their assumptions and to derive their recommendations logically from such assumptions. Until and unless this is done the field will remain one of limited psychological logic and recurrent fads.

I want to express my appreciation to Deborah Hudson, Carole Garlington, and Professors Jay W. Lorsch and Donald M. Levine for their help in the preparation of the manuscript.

HARRY LEVINSON

OTHER BOOKS BY HARRY LEVINSON

Men, Management, and Mental Health
Executive
Executive Stress
Organizational Diagnosis
The Great Jackass Fallacy
Emotional Health in the World of Work

These books may be ordered directly from:

The Levinson Institute, Inc.
Box 95
Cambridge, Mass. 02138

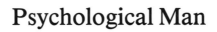

Psychological Man

Chapter 1

Psychoanalytic Principles of Personality Functioning

An executive, whether man or woman, is a leader of people. Either he builds an effective team, or he fails. As much as eighty percent of executive failure is due to the inability to lead, motivate, and integrate people toward the achievement of common purpose. As people become more affluent and better educated and therefore less likely to be motivated by money alone and more likely to be influenced by personal and professional standards, money and control, or carrot and stick, correspondingly lose whatever effectiveness they once may have had as motivational devices. Therefore, it is imperative for the executive to develop a sophisticated understanding of what motivates people. His knowledge about motivation must be as thorough as his knowledge of marketing, finance, control, policy, and production. Without it, he will be forced to rely on clichés, and he will flounder miserably, no matter how technically competent he may be, when he tries to act on the basis of that limited understanding.

It is important at the outset to understand that every managerial act, every organizational process and procedure makes some assumption about human motivation. An incentive system presumes that people are motivated by money. A name on the door and a rug on the floor reflects someone's assumption that people have powerful status aspirations. When a person talks to another about the prospect of promotion, he assumes that people want to advance in organizations. These assumptions may be valid in varying degrees or not at all. Certainly incentives offered by others are only part of a person's life experience, and their meaning to him depends on the rest of that experience. For example, to more fully understand economic factors in motivation we must know in greater depth their relevance to the feelings and thoughts of those to whom we offer them. Otherwise, we will be dismayed when such motivating efforts fail. Thus, we will want to look carefully at each managerial decision, each program, each step in organizing people to ask what underlying assumptions are being made and how valid they are.

People in organizations, by definition, work in groups, and these groups are organized into larger forms—sections, departments, divisions, companies, and so on. Executives necessarily must work with groups, often more than with individuals. There is a vast literature on group behavior ranging from small groups to large organizations. Social psychologists and sociologists have much to say about how groups function and how the executive might make use of that knowledge. However, these conceptions are based on tacit assumptions about what motivates individuals. In every statement about group behavior there are hidden beliefs about individual psychology. The executive who would make use of the behavioral sciences therefore should be prepared to examine what he or she reads and learns for its assumptions about the individual. Groups, after all, are made up of individuals. No one who does not understand individual behavior can fully understand group behavior or behavior in large organizational units.

Introduction

Of course, there are many forces which influence how a person feels, thinks, and behaves. People act differently when they are starving than when they are satiated, and differently when they are economically deprived than when they are affluent. A man or woman who operates an electron microscope alone goes about work differently than a person on an automobile assembly line. Economic, sociological, and technological considerations do make a difference in motivation and behavior.

The operation of these forces is relatively easy to observe and understand. But these forces interact with a complex set of forces going on within individuals which are much more obscure and more difficult to understand. It is foolhardy, if not dangerous, to assume that people are motivated by external forces alone, or even primarily by external forces. Furthermore, our understanding of external forces is, in most cases, too limited a base for predicting the likely behavior of individuals. We cannot predict how a given person will act in a specific situation under given conditions without knowing a great deal about that person. The executive places bets on just such predictions every time he or she selects, criticizes, or promotes a person. Therefore, we begin our effort to understand human behavior by a careful examination of individual motivation, or the functioning of the individual personality.

Why Theory? Unlike arms and legs, which may be measured, manipulated, observed, and even operated on, the most powerful internal motivating forces, feelings and thoughts, are not visible. We do not know what thoughts and feelings go on in people. We have to depend on what they tell us, or we have to make guesses from their behavior. Much of the time we cannot depend on what they say because few people want to share their innermost thoughts and feelings, and there are social constraints against expressing what we really feel. Besides, people often do not know why they behave as they do, or even what they are really feeling. Therefore, we need a theory to help us understand what goes on psychologically within the individual.

A theory is a series of interrelated concepts, or best guesses about what is going on in a given area. The better our theory about human behavior, the more efficiently it will enable us to understand and predict behavior. A good theory will help us to specify the reasons for the guesses or inferences we are making about motivation and give us an opportunity to test those guesses or hypotheses. By beginning with theory we develop the basis for processes of: (1) inference, or conclusion based on a guess or hypothesis; (2) test of the inference (was it the right guess?); (3) correction, based on feedback from behavior. A theory, therefore, is chiefly a mode of organizing one's thinking. It is a scientific device. It is not something one believes or doesn't believe. When a better theory comes along, the older one must be modified or abandoned.

Many people are uncomfortable about theory. They think of it as "long hair" or impractical or as something that only scientists use. Such feelings are especially prevalent in business circles. However, every one of us is always using theory. We do so in making assumptions about our everyday activities. A fisherman uses a theory about what level of the lake the fish are swimming in when he fixes his bobber on his line. A cook who is accustomed to boiling eggs in Boston discovers it takes longer to do so in the Rocky Mountains. Implicitly he or she had been using a theory about atmospheric pressure but didn't correct it in the new location. A parent is always using a theory when he or she disciplines a child, a supervisor when he or she communicates with a subordinate or a superior. Most of the time we can check our theories out quite readily in practice. However, when it comes to dealing with something as obscure as the sources of behavior, that more complex matter requires a more complex theory.

Which Theory? If a theory of personality is necessary, then which among the myriad of theories is the one to choose? Obviously a choice requires criteria. These—not necessarily original —are mine. One theory is better than another if:

(1) It leads to a better understanding, prediction, and control of behavior.
(2) It can account for and integrate the phenomena dealt with by another theory but not vice versa.
(3) It accounts for behavior from birth to death rather than one segment of life experience.
(4) It takes account of physiological, especially neurological, development.
(5) It accounts for unconscious motivation as well as conscious, for irrational behavior as well as the rational.
(6) It accounts for personality functioning in all settings, not

merely an occupation or school or home, as a systematic whole whose continuity is clearly recognizable.

(7) It accounts for the integration of mind and body, particularly for the relationship of emotions to physical processes, thereby explaining psychophysiological or psychosomatic symptoms.

(8) It accounts for interactional phenomena, the relationship of a person to other persons and to his environment, especially if it can account for how environmental forces create individual stress or, conversely, how they may be supportive of the individual personality.

(9) It leads to multiple avenues of research.

(10) Aspects of the theory are testable and modifiable as a result of research and experience.

(11) It provides a logic for intervention: for therapy if the personality is somehow impaired or injured; for education to enhance intellectual and emotional growth; for the psychological component of management, leadership, and professional practice in various disciplines.

(12) It answers the questions of "Why?" "What for?" to provide a logic for intervention and a choice of intervention methods based on the person, the problem, and the context.

(13) It serves as a consistent guide to managerial or professional behavior which has face validity, namely that in using the theory every day, one can verify for himself the degree to which it fits his daily experience and guides him in his everyday activities.

If we are to take a systems approach to person-in-organization, then we must also follow a systems approach to the person himself. Psychoanalytic theory is the only comprehensive theory of personality which seeks to understand, describe, and explain man's motivations and behavior from birth to death. It is the only theory to meet all of these criteria. It takes seriously the inner forces, both biological and psychological, which make man uniquely human. It conceives of these forces as subsystems of an integrated total system which we speak of as personality, and of that total system in interaction with its environment. It can include within its purview the concepts of the many other theories of personality but not vice versa.

It will, therefore, serve as our basic frame of reference. We can use it as a mode of integrating whatever else we may learn about personality, or as a point of departure for choosing whatever other conception might better fit our predilections and needs.

A System Conception. All living matter is embedded in a context. There are people who specialize in studying organisms in context. For example, ethologists are biologists who study animals in their natural habitat to understand the interrelationship of their sources of nourishment, protection, and other conditions for evolution and survival. Psychologists have tended to study aspects of people without taking their environments into account. Sociologists have tended to study environments without considering people as people; however, a person is a member of a family, a family is part of a kinship system and a neighborhood. The neighborhood is part of a community and the community of larger political and geographical units. The community has an economy, a geography, a topography, a population density, a given kind of school system and power structure. Although a person has a certain uniqueness—he will look like his parents and will develop into an adult human being regardless of environment—nevertheless, he is part of a system. We cannot really understand people and their behavior unless we take the system into account, too. Thus, as we talk about how men and women are motivated, we must necessarily also talk about the circumstances which have shaped them as well as the conditions under which they function.

Personality is the totality of the complex interaction of feelings, thoughts, and behavior as a series of interrelated subsystems and the whole as a system in equilibrium. A person is a system within a system. Therefore, personality has a dynamic structure. Since the personality is part of a living being who acts, we must conceive of a source of drive or energy which must be governed by some sort of *economic* principles. Obviously, a person obtains and stores information, only some of which he is aware of or can recall, so we must account for the *topography* of personality, or levels of awareness or consciousness. Just as obviously, the personality evolves from birth to death, so we must think of it as pursuing a *developmental* course. Finally, the personality copes with its environment; it maintains its balance or integrity and survives, which requires us to think of modes of *adaptation*. So we shall approach personality from these five points of view: dynamic, economic, topographic, developmental, and adaptive.

Before we begin to examine these points of view, let me clarify the relationship of heredity and the physiological side of man to personality. The human being is an animal. He has certain inherited physical traits, capacities, and limitations. That is, we inherit such qualities as the color of our hair, the size of our nose, the physique of our bodies, and other physical traits. A person who has inherited an extraordinary capacity for fine motor coordination may have the necessary talents to become an excellent baseball player. He does not inherit the skill of playing baseball but he does inherit "the makings." A look at newborn infants in a hospital nursery will disclose that, from birth, some are calm and placid and others are easily irritable and more highly sensitive. Each person from birth differs both in his particular combination of natural endowments and in the degree to which these permit him to contend with various aspects of life. A person born with above average intelligence certainly will be able to deal with the problems of living with considerably greater ease than the person who is born retarded. A naturally phlegmatic person will tend to be less aroused when stimulated by the irritants of life than one who tends to respond more quickly to stimulation.

Heredity to a large extent determines what a person will be in the sense that he or she cannot be anything other than a two-legged, two-eyed, ten-fingered person. There are degrees of intelligence among us, various physiques and differential sensitivity to what each person sees, feels, hears, and touches. Some of us are short, some tall, some have handicaps, some have particular gifts.

We do not know as much about inherited abilities and capacities as we would like to know, and we are rather vague about just how much inherited or constitutional factors have to do with psychological motivation. In this book we shall be discussing primarily the psychological side of man. This does not mean that we ignore his physical or biological side, but rather that we are not prepared to speak as comprehensively about its relationship to motivation as we are about the psychological aspect of his being.

A Five-Part Conception of Personality

1. Dynamic Viewpoint. Structurally, following Freud, we can divide the personality into three major parts. One part we call the *id*. The word *id* is a label for a group of functions and processes which are arbitrarily lumped together for better understanding. We speak as if it were a thing, but it is only a concept. The id is the seat of many memories and experiences which we cannot recall, and of the instinctual drives about which we shall talk later. Few of us can remember many experiences which happened before we were five years old. Many of the other experiences which have happened to us since are no longer in memory. Yet most of these events can be recalled under hypnosis or various forms of drugs or in certain kinds of illnesses. These experiences are stored within us as data are stored in the disc or tape of a computer or sound is recorded on a tape recorder. These experiences have had some effect on us and, in fact, continue to have an effect on us because they continue to exist, though well beyond our awareness. We allocate to the id also primitive urges and drives, that animal part of us which has been subdued, organized and controlled, but not obliterated, by the socializing effects of civilization.

The *ego*, a concept which designates the executive part of the personality, includes thinking and judgment, attention, concentration, perception, and planning. We have an organized intellectual and emotional life. We are able to understand and interpret many of the things which happen to us in the course of the day. We can remember incidents which happened to us yesterday and we can recall many events of the years gone by. To the ego we allocate the more rational planning and controlling functions of the person. It is that part of the personality which deals more directly with reality. In contrast, the id is largely

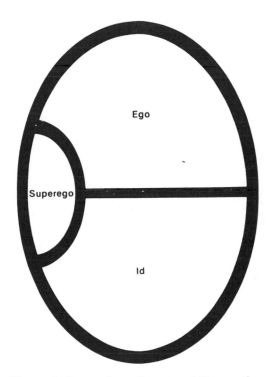

**Figure 1. Dynamic or Structural Conception:
A View of the Personality**

irrational. The ego is governed by what Freud called the reality principle—it takes into account external reality for the long-run survival of the organism. The id is governed by what he calls the pleasure principle—basic urges and drives seek gratification regardless of consequences. Thus, these forces in the id must be controlled, guided, and directed by the ego. The ego also controls the muscles and body organs—the capacity to act on environment or self.

An extremely important component of the structural aspect of the theory is the differentiation between primary process and secondary process thinking. Primary process thinking is characteristic of small children, often of primitive people, and occurs in normal adults in dreams. It seems to follow no apparent logic, at least not the rational logic characteristic of most adults in our society. It is often magical, condensed, symbolic, and without a time dimension: in dreams, events which have happened some years apart may seem as if they had happened sequentially. A small child has no difficulty accepting the idea that Santa Claus can descend from a sleigh pulled by flying reindeer into millions of chimneys with sufficient toys for all the children of the world in one night. By the time the child is five, he begins to doubt; by six, the idea is absurd. Rational, secondary process thinking has gained supremacy.

Primary process is not limited to children. Psychiatrist Michael A. Simpson asked seventy-eight medical, nursing, and theological students in a university course to fill out their own death certificates, guessing the date and cause of their deaths.[1] Some felt unable to fill them out at all; some filled them in but refused to let anyone see them; two returned them but asked that they be burned. Only thirty students turned in their certificates! Why all this feeling? The fear that writing it down might make it come true—word magic, a feature of primary process thinking.

As intelligent adults immersed in rational pursuits, we are usually unaware of our primary process or irrational side. Consequently, we neglect to take the irrational into account in managing. The primary process thinking of childhood does not disappear as we grow up. It is merely overlaid with rational processes. Indeed, even Freud was superstitious about his death date. Magical thinking surfaces when we feel threatened or feel we might be threatening someone else. It lays an extra emotional burden on us.

Our major concern with primary process thinking is that a thought, feeling, or wish is equated with the act by the child. As we saw in the death certificate example, to think something is the same as to do it. This raises particularly difficult problems when it comes to dealing with feelings of anger or hostility. All children become angry with their parents and siblings. If to become angry and to wish the temporary enemy destroyed unconsciously is the same as to do it, then in his fantasy the child runs the risk of losing the parents on whom he depends, of being viewed as bad, and of being punished on the talion principle—an eye for an eye. Such fantasies may cause the child to lean over backwards not to display anger, to deny his anger, and to feel guilty for such thoughts as if they were indeed behavior. Secondary process thinking is the normal rational process of thinking we know as adults. As secondary process thinking develops, as I noted in the example above, it does not entirely wipe out primary process thinking. As a result we tend to feel disproportionately and irrationally guilty for feelings of hostility. This guilt in turn corrupts the ability to supervise and appraise others and frequently leads to managerial actions which are guided more by the unconscious wish to avoid guilt than by rational managerial needs.

The third aspect of the structure of the personality which we conceptualize we label as the conscience, or *superego*. The superego is an acquired and developed structure, not an inherited one. The superego incorporates the moral and spiritual values of the culture in which a person lives, the rules and regulations within the family, and the attitudes toward himself which the person has acquired from those around him. Thus the superego is at once a policeman, a judge, and a preceptor. The superego represents the law, telling us what we should or should not do. It represents the judiciary, in judging how well we conform to the rules which it has set up, and it represents the preceptor, incorporating values and aspirations and goals. The person who has a strong superego has a long list of rules which he feels he must obey. Many of these are unconscious and therefore not in his awareness at all.

There are modes of thinking and behaving an adult takes for granted, having learned them as a child. If, however, he does not think or behave in those ways, he feels guilty and unhappy and uncomfortable. Since some of the admonitions have become unconscious, a person may no longer be aware of why he continues to feel unhappy and uncomfortable.

A superego that is not an extreme one, which does not have so many rules that a person cannot enjoy life, serves as an important guide and protector. By telling us what is right and wrong for us, by making us aware of possible punishments should we violate the rules, and by punishing us with guilt for infractions, the superego keeps us on the straight and narrow path, so to speak. It should be noted again that although we speak of the superego as if it were a thing, it is only a concept, a way of grouping certain feelings and thoughts.

An important part of the superego is the *ego ideal*, or our image of ourselves at our future best. The ego ideal is a lifetime road map. We feel guilty if we are not working toward its ends. A person's wish to meet the demands of his own ego ideal, to be able to like himself, is the most powerful of all motivational forces. *Self-esteem* is reflected in the gap between the ego ideal and the self-image, or one's views of how things are in the present. If we were to measure ego ideal and self-image, this relationship might be expressed mathematically as follows:

$$self\text{-}esteem = \frac{1}{ego\ ideal - self\text{-}image}$$

Thus, if the ego ideal were given a value of 10 and the self-image a value of 5, self-esteem would have a value of .2. If ego ideal were 20 and self-image 5, self-esteem would then be .066. The closer one approaches his ego ideal, the better he likes himself. Conversely, the greater the gap, the angrier one becomes with himself. Self-directed anger results in depression.

The ego ideal differs from the common understanding of the concept of self-actualization. The latter refers to the fulfillment of one's potential. Humanistic psychologists hold that failure to actualize oneself or to fulfill potential causes problems for the individual. According to our conception, potential is irrelevant. A person may have the potential to be an atomic physicist but may have a vastly different ego ideal. Unless he meets the demands of his own ego ideal, he is likely to be angry with himself. The ego ideal is partly culturally determined, but highly individualized.

We all know of people whose consciences would give them no peace for violations, and who therefore must atone constantly for what they believe to be errors or sin, or for not doing well enough. A conscience, if too rigid and too punitive, can make a person feel unduly guilty, ashamed, or worthless. If childhood experiences were full of restrictions and punishments, if everything a child did was viewed as bad and he was constantly reminded of his inadequacies, his picture of himself is hardly likely to be one of a worthwhile, good person. His conscience may serve then as a harsh whip throughout his life. Those familiar with transactional analysis will recognize the "child," the "parent," and the "adult" to be popular representations of the id, superego, and ego.

2. Economic Viewpoint. An organism needs not only structure but motivational power as well. Biochemically two forces operate continuously in all plants and animals. There is a constructive or growth force called anabolism which works concurrently with a destructive or decomposition force called catabolism. Cells are constantly being created and destroyed. In the early life of any organism the anabolic forces are greater, and the organism grows and develops. In the later stages of the age of any organism, the catabolic forces gain dominance, and ultimately the organism declines and dies. The processes, however, continue concurrently throughout a lifetime. We see this most simply physiologically with injuries. A child who breaks an arm or a leg usually recovers quickly. Elderly adults necessarily fear a fall because recovery from a broken limb is a long, arduous process.

Freudian theorists assume that two basic psychological drives derive from this dual process of growth and destruction, of life and death: sex and aggression, which are sometimes called the constructive and destructive drives, or the life and death instincts. The basic feelings of love and hate derive from these drives. A major psychological task in one's life is to so fuse constructive and destructive drives that they serve himself and society rather than destructive ends.

Drives give rise to feelings, feelings to thoughts, and thoughts to behavior. This sequence modulates the effects of the drives and makes self-control possible. This sequence also means that if we would understand behavior we must work backwards from the behavior to the thoughts that preceded it and further to the feelings which gave rise to the thoughts.

The aggressive drive is the force which makes us want to strike out when we are frustrated or angry or hurt. It is that force which gives us the motive power for defending ourselves against attack and the energy or drive which we invest in our various tasks. In early life the infant responds to frustration with anger or rage. The child must learn that he cannot go around striking, demanding, and hurting.

Early in life the constructive drive, the life instinct if you will, may appear to be selfish and pleasure seeking, with direct self-preservation as its primary aim. An infant tries to obtain food, warmth, and affection from those around him for his own survival. As it becomes more refined, however, the constructive drive becomes a source of thoughts and actions that are loving, kind, and creative.

In its rawest form, the aggressive drive expresses itself in mean and destructive feelings, thoughts, and actions. When people fail to grow up emotionally, when we see adults whom we speak of as immature, we mean that they act selfishly. They neglect themselves and others, they put off what they ought to do to fulfill their responsibilities, they are more readily jealous of others, and they are evidently hostile to others. However, when the aggressive drive is tempered by and balanced with the constructive drive, the aggressive drive serves as the energy to conquer the obstructions which stand in the way of reaching worthwhile goals. Well-coordinated, these two forces are both manifest in the achievement of successful business careers, of the gratification of a wide range of recreational activities, of good family and interpersonal relationships, and so on.

The constructive and destructive drives work like gasoline and oxygen in an automobile engine. Mixed together in the right amounts, gasoline and oxygen make the car work well. If there is too much gas, the engine floods and potential energy is wasted. If there is too much oxygen, the engine sputters and stops. If there is too much aggressive energy that is poorly directed and controlled, then it is not only wasted but also destructive. If there is not enough of it, then a person lacks drive and ambition.

The major psychological task for all of us is to learn to balance these two drives in our own best interests and in the best interest of society. How we do so depends very much on our

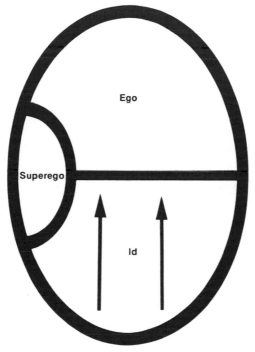

(Sex)   Constructive/Destructive Drives   (Aggression)

**Figure 2. Economic or Energetic Conception:
The Energy Sources of the Personality**

early childhood experiences. If in the course of our early development our aggressive feelings were heavily stimulated by undue hostility on the part of others, powerful unconscious fantasies, or undue frustration, then we may have too much poorly controlled, accumulated aggression, which may get out of hand. If, however, during that same period of time we were given much love, consideration, and attention, this would tend to strengthen the constructive forces in the personality and make them better able to control the destructive forces. If a person's needs are adequately met, if he is given opportunity to express his feelings freely, his original self-centered concern grows into love for other people who have demonstrated their love for him. In its more mature form, the constructive drive expresses itself in the creation of and love for a family, and in adding and giving something to the world. Of course, sometimes the interests of the person are opposed to those of society. Slavery was an example. In such instances energy must be invested in social reform or compromises.

These two psychological drives operate simultaneously and unconsciously. We are unaware of their continuous functioning. We can't measure them quantitatively, so this part of the theory is most hotly debated. Many people do not accept the concept of inherited aggression. However, animal studies seem to bear it out. [2]

3. Topographic Viewpoint. Topography refers to levels of consciousness. We are aware of many things going on around us—noise, movement, other people, and so forth. To be *conscious* or aware is to focus attention immediately. However, we are not immediately aware of many things, many experiences. We do not think of what happened to us yesterday, or we forget a name. We can at will recall the former and may spontaneously recall the latter at a later time. We speak of such phenomena and experiences as *preconscious*, meaning they are available to consciousness.

However, there are many experiences we cannot recall even if we want to, no matter how hard we try. Some are recallable under anesthesia, hypnosis, psychoanalysis, and similar circumstances. These we speak of as *unconscious*. People's personalities are shaped significantly by events of their past and fantasies about them which they can no longer recall because these events and the fantasies about them constitute the person's experience with his world and his interpretation of those experiences. These become the basis for his understanding of himself and his environment. For example, a child of divorced parents may well feel he is responsible for the divorce because of his rivalry with the father. The consequent guilt and disappearance of the father may make him feel worthless and subject to abandonment.

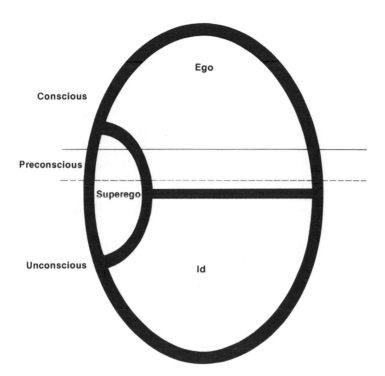

**Figure 3. Topographic Conception:
Levels of Awareness of the Personality**

4. Developmental Viewpoint. The fact that the organism grows from being a helpless infant to a mature adult means that it passes through a pattern of development. During this pattern of development it is at different times capable of behaving differently. Ways of thinking, modes of forming concepts, the use of the musculature, coordination—all of these change with time, and these changes are influenced by experience. We are not as we were in the beginning, and indeed, as those who wear bifocals will testify, our flexibility tends to deteriorate a bit with age.

In that sense man is no different from a tree. One can bend a sapling, shape it, twist it, but one is less able to do that as it becomes bigger and thicker and stronger because it also becomes more rigid.

Freud observed that the child experienced a series of stages in development which had much to do with his physiological development. As a child grows, he gets pleasure or gratification from different parts of his body at different times. This observation was the basis for his theory of psychosexual development. In this conception sexual simply refers to gratification from any part of the body. But the idea that children have sexual interests, however broadly the term is used, disturbed many people and still does. Most people do not understand the physiological facts underlying his formulation.

A complementary theory of psychosocial development has been formulated by Erik H. Erikson which will be discussed later. Erikson specifies the crucial social relationships and experiences which occur at each stage in the psychosexual development.

In roughly the first eighteen months of his development, the child is oriented around his mouth; that is, he must eat to survive, and at that time, the nerve endings of the mouth are more highly refined than those anywhere else. Therefore, in addition to being oriented around the mouth for eating purposes, the infant takes pleasure or gets gratification from the use of the mouth. This can be tested in animal experiments. For example, if one feeds puppies through a bottle with a nipple that has large holes punched in it so that the milk flows easily and the puppies get the milk without chewing and sucking on the nipple, subsequently the puppies will chew on each other's ears. Puppies who are fed with the usual kind of nipple without the large holes in it don't chew on each other.

Observe, also, that most adults use the mouth beyond what is needed to take in minimally necessary food. We smoke, we chew gum, we enjoy talking, we become epicureans, we may like good wines or special flavors or something else like that, and there is continued pleasure in the use of the mouth. We can use the mouth to express love and affection, as in kissing or speaking affectionate or supportive words, or we can use it aggressively or in hostile fashion by attacking somebody else, by biting. We talk about making biting remarks, destroying somebody's reputation with gossip, and similar acts of oral aggression. Thus, both drives continuously operate through all developmental phases. In his earliest state of helplessness the child is completely dependent on the parents or parent figures. The child may react to this helplessness by experiencing the outside world as hostile and painful, in which case he is likely to adopt a *paranoid* or suspicious attitude toward the perceived hostile world and adapt to it by a fighting posture. Or he may experience himself as inadequate and worthless and therefore adopt a *depressive* attitude, or one which depreciates himself and assumes himself to be blameworthy for the inadequacies of his situation.[3] Between these polar extremes are many shadings. These basic positions may be either amplified or modified by subsequent experiences.

The helpless child, seeking to become less helpless, begins to acquire competence by identifying with the closest more competent models, namely parents or parent figures. From the vantage point of the child, they are omnipotent. Seeking the same omnipotence, the child emulates their behavior and incorporates his perception of their perfect images within himself. Implicitly, such identification and incorporation include the experience of rivalry. That is, wanting to be just as good as, if not better than, they, the child takes from them elements of their behavior which ultimately make him as strong as, if not stronger than, they. Psychological growth is based significantly on models.

Thus, there is the continuous need to emulate power figures, to identify with them, and to acquire their competence. In addition, of course, the child experiences protection, nurture, love, security, and those other elements of the bonding process which facilitate the establishment of a relationship through which the child can acquire the behavior of the parent.

Identification is not acquired without rivalry or elements of rejection. The child also experiences fear, rage, and other negative feelings which make all relationships ambivalent. To be completely helpless and utterly dependent on the parent is to be merely an extension of the parent. That does not relieve the feelings of helplessness.

Roughly in the next eighteen months (these stages will overlap and this is not a rigid schedule) is the anal stage of development. At this time the nerve endings of the anus become highly refined, and for the first time the child has his attention called to the functions of excretion. Notice that this occurs at a time when the child discovers that he has something that somebody else wants; otherwise, why would people pay so much attention to it? And if one gives when he's supposed to be giving, mother is highly pleased. If he gives with regularity, she is pleased that he's trained. If he doesn't give, then she becomes exasperated and very unhappy. He then discovers that he has a device which has the capacity of exasperating mother, a weapon for getting back at her. So the whole issue of giving or withholding has to do with the development of the capacity to hold on tight or to let go and give out. There are contemporary continuities of this. We speak of people who are miserly as "tight." We speak about money as "filthy lucre." Once again, positive and negative, or affectionate and aggressive, drives are expressed in this stage.

One begins to see, particularly in two-year-olds, the child's rebellion against parental wishes, controls, and dicta and the pressure toward autonomy. Angry feelings begin to rise to consciousness. In this period, if the child represses and overcontrols his feelings, he is always threatened by the potential loss of control. This kind of internal pressure gives added weight to his feeling of helplessness and the depressive position. The child is then more likely to build rigid controls around himself. If, on the other hand, the child continues to fight a perceived hostile and oppressive world, his experience gives added emphasis to the paranoid position. Subsequent adult occupational choice and leadership behavior may frequently be compensations for the unconscious feelings of helplessness and the conflicts around those feelings which were exacerbated at certain points in development. For example, some people are driven to acquire power to cope with their feelings of having been victimized by a cruel world. As politicians or tycoons they seek to control as much of their environments as they can to reduce their feelings of vulnerability. Richard Nixon frequently spoke of the pain of his impoverished childhood. His history was one of pursuing power.

The third stage of psychosexual development according to Freudian theory, roughly between ages three and six, is the phallic stage, at which time nerve endings of the sex organs become highly refined, and children discover their sexual differences. Up to this point boys and girls have played together without caring too much about the distinction between them. Now children become aware of the fact that there are pleasurable sensations in those parts of the body. Once again the full force of social power may impinge upon them in the form of criticism about touching or playing with their sexual organs. In our culture, until relatively recently, condemnation of sexual curiosity, interest, and play produced widespread guilt around sexuality in adults.

The discovery of sexual differences is a painful experience, one which we have tended to pass over because it is too painful to remember. It is difficult for children to accept the fact that there is a difference between them. Up to this point they have played together and the difference has not existed for all practical purposes. Suddenly the difference makes a difference. How does one explain it? Little girls will ask, "Why am I not like brother?" Or they may insist that they will in time grow a penis. When the parent says, "No, you're a girl, you will not," they have considerable difficulty accepting this. Boys, on the other hand, are very fearful about the difference because if they have a penis, what happened to the one she had? She must have had one; everybody has one, they reason. It makes no sense to them that only some have one. So something must have happened to it; it must have been cut off, or something else equally punitive must have happened. Therefore, a certain kind of fear arises in boys with this discovery, a fear sometimes so powerful that later they are reluctant to assert themselves as men. Many girls are unwilling to accept the difference. These girls indulge in various kinds of tomboy behavior until the time of menstruation, when it becomes physiologically clear that they are not going to change; they are indeed feminine. Some women never seem to get over what they feel to have been a deprivation. They go through life trying to prove to themselves that they are not female. Some men have equally great difficulty with sexual identification as widely publicized sex-change operations indicate. The phallic stage, then, is a very, very difficult period for children.

The next stage, roughly from six to twelve or so, is called the latency period. The concern for sexuality becomes quiescent. Boys concentrate on being boys and girls on being girls. They want nothing to do with each other. With the onset of puberty, children reach the genital stage. Physiologically, they are capable of procreation. They begin to reestablish relationships with the other sex.

Now, let us return to the phallic stage because there is an additional very critical issue. This is what is referred to as the "Oedipus complex" from the Greek myth. Oedipus was, according to the story, a prince. The Delphic oracle told his father that his son would rise up and kill him. So the son was abandoned in the fashion of Moses. (Notice the repetition of this kind of myth in different cultures. The contemporary reincarnation is Superman.) He was rescued, reared by a neighboring king, and subsequently became a prince again. He engaged in combat with his father, without knowing his opponent's real identity, and destroyed him. He then successfully answered the riddle of the Sphinx. His reward was the widow of the king he had slain. Oedipus discovered subsequently that he had married his own mother. He then blinded himself and, driven from Thebes by his sons, died in poverty and exile. Thus, he violated the only two universal taboos: parricide and incest.

Freud observed, as have many others who have worked with children, that there comes a point in time when children are rivalrous with the parent of the same sex for the attention and affection of the parent of the opposite sex. Children will try to get in bed with their parents and separate them. They try to demand the attention of the parent of the opposite sex to the exclusion of the one of the same sex. This becomes a psychologically painful battle because the child soon discovers, if he happens to be a boy, that father is far more powerful and he had better not fight too hard or father might retaliate. This conflict arises at a point when the child is already worried about what happened to the lost penis of the girl. When fears and threats become exaggerated in fantasy, the little boy assumes that this massively powerful enemy can really castrate him. This rivalry and potential threat must be resolved. Ideally it is resolved on the principle that if you can't lick him, you join him. This then creates the conditions for identification, for taking in the parent and making him part of oneself. This is the chip-off-the-old-block phenomenon. The little boy, discovering that he cannot have mother because father has mother, comes to the conclusion that the next best course is to be like father, in which case he may get somebody who is like mother. Thus, by identifying with father, he crystallizes the outlines of his character formation. He becomes much like the parent, not only physiologically but in terms of his behavior, as was noted earlier. Sometimes when one sees a father and son walking together, talking together, they seem almost identical. Indeed, it is a compliment to the father when the son emulates him.

Little girls at this point in time have the same problems that little boys have trying to explain to themselves why they do not have the same sexual organs as little boys. Some in their fantasy will assume this to be because they have been bad and therefore their sexual organs have been taken away as punishment, or that they are less than adequate because something is missing in them. These infantile fantasies are reinforced in many cultures— indeed even in our own until fairly recently—by sexual- and social-role stereotyping which communicates to girls that they are not as good as boys. They are "the weaker sex." Thus, elements of truth are given to otherwise irrational fantasies. These social definitions of women often tended to undermine their self-images, to make them take a more dependent role and to be more reluctant to compete with men. Some would try to compensate for these self-images by overasserting their denial of them, striving to be more like strong men than what they perceived to be weak women.

Both parents are powerful role models for children of both sexes. In the identification process children incorporate parental values, parental behaviors, and parental expectations. Children abstract the major characteristics of the parents with whom they identify, particularly the parent of the same sex, to evolve their occupational choices. The oedipal experience, however, is such a painful one that the child represses it, pushes it out of consciousness and with it everything that came before, which is why we have great difficulty remembering what happened to us before we were five or six years old.

The oedipal struggle is so critical that it is conducive to difficulties and malformation of personality development. For example, if there are severe frictions between mother and father, and either of them says in effect or directly, "Don't be like him (her)," or if it becomes clear to the child that one has no use for the other, there is no point in identifying with him (her). That will not lead to success in obtaining the affection of the other. In fact, the child will be more successful in obtaining affection if he or she does not identify fully. In such circumstances a boy may often seek the mother as a substitute for the rejected father, which makes for distortion in growing up. If he experiences father as unduly harsh, it will be extremely difficult to identify with him; thus the unconscious rivalry is continued.

If the daughter feels her mother to be weak or somehow inadequate she may not want to identify with such a helpless figure and may instead identify with her father. This is especially likely to be true if her infantile fantasies have led her to believe that she is incomplete because something is missing. Her rivalry may be intensified if she perceives that father likes her better than he likes mother or if she interprets some aspect of his behavior as giving her indication that she might win out in the competition for him.

Where the mother is the only permanent figure and there may be a series of adult men moving through the family, the male child has little opportunity to identify with a man who demonstrates responsibility for the family and earns a livelihood. There is, then, a vacuum of male identification possibilities, making the evolution of a role model difficult. To the extent to which there are inadequate role models for the girls, the same problem may arise. In addition, without an adequate paternal figure the girl has no male model to use as a basis for selecting a mate or for pursuing occupational roles other than those defined as feminine.

In lower-class families the pressure toward achievement usually comes from the mother, who wants something more for her children. She often encourages, indeed pushes, the child to better himself. At lower socioeconomic levels it is often the father who says, "I only went to the eighth grade. What do you have to get more education for?" The mother will say, "You need more, you want more, you should want more," and pushes the child along. In the middle classes, both parents push. When both parents are in agreement, this consolidates the child's identification. Otherwise there may well be conflict within the ego ideal which undermines the possibility of moving the self-image toward the ego ideal and of consistent pursuit of career. We will explore the issue of parental influence on occupational choice later.

As the child incorporates the parental images within himself, he identifies not only with the behavior of the parents, but more importantly with their ego ideals. That is, viewing them as omnipotent, he identifies not with the parents as they really are, but as he perceives them to be, including the values and rules they espouse but do not necessarily live up to. Thus, through the identification process, a child builds a powerful set of self-demands in the form of an ego ideal far beyond his competence, which means that he has a self-image of inadequacy. With much love, affection, and support the inadequacy may be appropriately tempered, and the child may develop a more realistic ego ideal and an improved self-image. With greater disciplinary pressure the ego ideal may become more distant and the self-image lower, increasing the sense of inadequacy.

When in the oedipal stage the intensity of the rivalry is increased, the child, dependent on primary process or magical thinking, becomes even more fearful of what he imagines to be the potential destructiveness of his own angry impulses. This makes him feel all the more unworthy and unlovable. Therefore, it becomes all the more necessary to facilitate the identification process with love and affection in order for the child to have a core image of himself as a lovable person around which he can then build his self-image and subsequently his career goals. For women the same issues hold true. We know that successful women executives were nurtured and encouraged, not only by mothers, teachers, and others who served as good identification models and who fostered their free-ranging occupational choices, but also by fathers who held them in esteem, nurtured their self-images, and encouraged them to combine both masculine and feminine identifications.

Taken together, all this constitutes the theory of psychosexual development, which explains how the fundamental outlines of the personality are formed very early in life. By the time the Oedipus conflict is resolved there are also formidable bits of superego. Of course, the superego continues to develop through a lifetime, as indeed does the ego. But the outlines are pretty well established as a result of identification with parents.

The superego tends to be more severe for boys than it is for girls because boys are compelled to resolve the oedipus complex at a much earlier age than girls. Both boys and girls identify first with the mother, then with the father. Boys must crystallize their identification at that point if they are to emulate their fathers and become men. They must cope with their powerful rivalrous feelings, and their hostility, and introject the paternal values at a time when they are too young to fully understand their feelings and identifications. Girls usually do not modify the wish to identify with the father and return to identifying more fully with the mother until puberty. By that time they are more mature and have a more accurate perspective on themselves, their parents, their feelings, and the values they accept.

Obviously the superego for many women is indeed severe or there would be no depressions or suicides among them. High expectations on the part of the parents for good behavior or academic performance, heavy control, and the manipulation of guilt feelings by the parents, together with unconscious guilt for feelings of hostility, all can combine to increase the severity of the superego for girls just as they can and do for boys.

Following Freud's work tracing the psycho-physiological aspects of development and their impact on the formation of personality, Erik H. Erikson developed a complementary conception, a psychosocial pattern of development encompassing the whole life cycle.[4]

Figure 4. Developmental Conception:
The Growth and Formation of the Personality

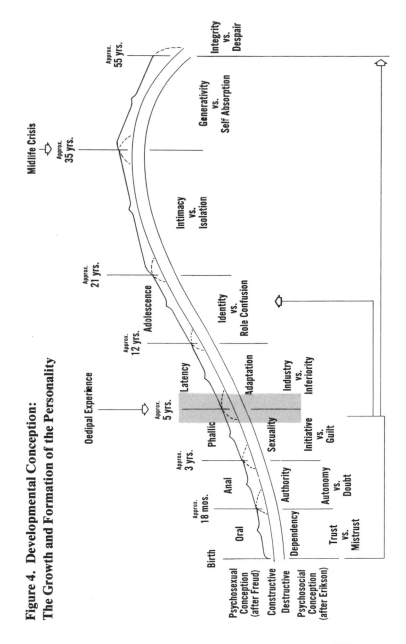

Referring to the helplessness, and therefore the complete dependency, of the child, Erikson observes that in the oral stage the child learns to trust or to mistrust people in his environment depending on how well and consistently his parents meet his needs. Dependency and helplessness are difficult to tolerate. Each of us seeks to escape from that condition as rapidly as possible. Yet we all need to depend on others. A conflict about dependency endures for a lifetime. Some people cannot let themselves depend on others; some have difficulty standing alone. Most of us are in between, but we all struggle with these feelings.

During the anal stage, the infant comes face to face with authority and its demands. Mother tries to teach him bowel and bladder control, and sometimes tries to compel him to obey. This is his first experience with the full force of social control. The child struggles for autonomy against feelings of shame and doubt. Ideally the child should learn self-control without loss of self-esteem, but often he is abused or shamed into good behavior. Parental overcontrol brings a lasting sense of doubt and shame. The fundamental conflict is with authority, and here the child begins to evolve ways of coping with authority.

The phallic stage is characterized by the conflict between initiative and guilt. The child is curious, interested in, and over-concerned with his sexual discoveries. If he is made to feel guilty about these interests, then guilt will contribute to inhibition. Ideally his curiosity should stimulate initiative and his comfortable establishment of himself in his sex role. The issue here is, "Can I develop my interests and skills in whatever direction I want and still be in keeping with what constitutes a man (woman) in this culture?"

In the latency period the child concentrates on adaptation. He or she learns skills and develops competences. He learns to master things and fantasies by work and play, by experimenting, sharing, and planning. At this stage he develops either a feeling of adequacy or one of inferiority.

In adolescence, the central issue is identity. Ideally, the young person now begins to integrate all of his experiences toward a defined personality within a social reality. Here issues of dependency, authority, and sexuality recur. The critical questions are:

"Who am I? What am I? Where am I going?" Implicit in the concern with identity is, "Do I stand up and stand on my own, or do I lean on my parents?" On the one hand, the pleasures, security, and warmth of the family are welcome; on the other, "I want to grow up and be an adult. Hurry up, let me grow up." Life pulls in both directions.

The next question is, "Who is boss around here? Do I do what you want me to do, or what I want to do?" A ten-year-old girl said, "In eight years you won't be able to boss me anymore." She only began to say what is going to come, for in a few more years her feeling will grow in intensity. Then there will be sharper issues about who is going to be boss. In addition, the issue of sexuality is reawakened: "Am I a man or not a man (or woman)? What does it take to be a man (woman)?"

From this point on, all of these reawakened feelings are present. Dependency, authority, sexuality, and feelings about them enter into every kind of relationship, including those in the business world. They will be found in every supervisory problem, in every personality conflict, and in every managerial decision.

Erikson went beyond Freud to define three additional stages of adulthood, testifying to the fact that we continue to change psychologically as we grow older. Although the outlines of personality are laid down early, personality is by no means fixed at the five-year level. Development continues.

The first stage of adulthood is characterized by a conflict between intimacy and isolation. Ideally the young adult establishes real intimacy with a person of the other sex, and with other people, for that matter. He is able to come close to others if some problem does not require him to withdraw or push them away. Having established intimacy, the adult moves on to generativity. This concerns the establishment of the next generation. Individuals who do not develop generativity, Erikson says, often begin to indulge themselves as if they were their own one and only child. Finally, the last stage is characterized by the development of integrity. According to Erikson, it is an acceptance of one's own and only life cycle and of the people who have become significant to it as something that had to be. He adds that the lack or loss of this accrued ego integration (the bringing together of the self-image and the ego ideal) is signified by despair and often an unconscious fear of death: the one and only life cycle is not accepted as the ultimate of life.

So there are many psychological tasks to accomplish from birth to death. These arise from within the person and are accomplished through interaction with the environment, particularly in relationships with significant other people. As Erikson points out, these tasks are never completely resolved. Every person is always working on them. A person's work and the conditions under which he does it are important modes of accomplishing these essential psychological tasks.

The fundamental elements in male occupational choice are father's values (his ego ideal) and the extent to which those together with father's behavior as a male adult pleased mother. In fact, the single most crucial element in occupational choice for the boy is what pleases mother, and for the girl what pleases father. The greater the conflict between the parents around these issues and the greater the difficulty of identification, the more difficulty there will be in occupational choice.

5. Adaptive Viewpoint. Thus far we have spoken of a biological organism which also has a psychology—feelings, thoughts, and behavior. The psychological aspect of the organism has both primitive and civilized components. Some feelings and thoughts are conscious, some unconscious. We have seen how conscience or superego develops and then becomes a force operating on the ego. We have also seen something of the operation of constructive and destructive drives, whose integration becomes a major task for the ego. In addition to these two internal forces—the superego and the id (including the drives)—man through his ego has to deal with external forces.

At times a person's environment is a source of affection, support, and security. The child in his mother's arms, a man enjoying himself among his friends, a man or woman in a happy marriage, a person building a business, a teacher helping others to learn, or a minister serving his congregation all draw emotional nourishment from the environment. Such nourishment strengthens the constructive forces of the personality.

When looked at closely, needs for status and esteem are essentially needs for love and affection. Few can survive long without giving and receiving love, though often in ways which are disguised. We know from studies of infants, concentration camp survivors, and the aging that relationships with other human beings literally make a life-or-death difference. Without relationships people become ill more often, deteriorate more quickly, give up more easily, and lose their reason for living. This is a major reason why people strive so hard to attain positions and possessions which become devices for obtaining the admiration, and presumably the regard, of others. Status needs have to do with the constructive forces of the personality. When a man seeks symbols of status, he simply searches for some concrete indication that some others hold him in esteem, or, more fundamentally, love him. A person needs infusions of affection and gratification to foster his own strength. Unfortunately, status is inadequate as a substitute for affection, and therefore the need for status is insatiable when a person depends on his status alone for his self-esteem.

The environment may also stimulate aggression: anger, jealousy, exploitation, competition for various advantages, economic reverses, wars, and so on. Every person must deal with the realities of his environment—the necessity of earning a livelihood, the frustration of an unsolved problem, the achievement of personal goals, or the development of satisfying relationships with other people.

The ego is always engaged in the task of balancing these multiple forces to maintain the equilibrium of the personality as an integrated system. To do this balancing task, man has a built-in psychological stabilizing force which operates in a way analogous to a gyroscope in a ship or airplane. This stabilizing factor has two components: *anxiety;* and *defense,* or *coping mechanisms.*

When for some reason the personality is threatened with imbalance, danger signals arise which take the form of anxiety. Anxiety is a state of internal alarm which causes the organism to mobilize its resources to protect itself. Anxiety is like fever in that respect. It is necessary for survival but too much of it may

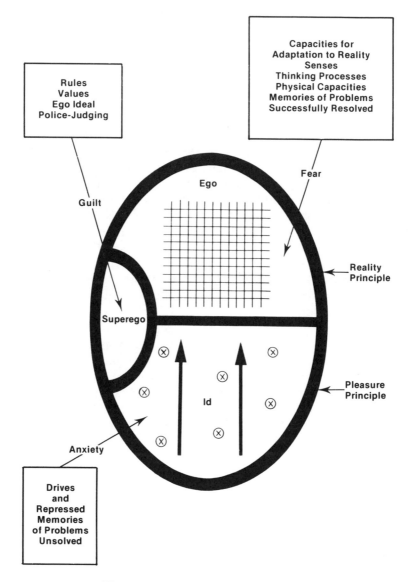

**Figure 5. Adaptational Conception I:
The Equilibrium-Maintaining Activities
of the Personality**

itself be threatening. There are three kinds of anxiety: *fear,* or conscious awareness of external danger; *guilt,* or threat from the superego (the major problem in occupational stress); and *anxiety proper,* or the unconscious fear of being overwhelmed by pressures from the id and, as a result, falling apart or losing control of oneself.

In response to anxiety, the ego has certain defense mechanisms, or standard methods for protecting the personality. *Identification,* the process of emulation, is a basic way of building one's own personality. Identifications may be temporary, as when a child imitates a movie star or athlete or a subordinate dresses as his boss does. Identifications may shift from one model to another, or a person may identify with only some of the skills, competences, and values of another. All of us seek to emulate the best qualities of those we admire. Sometimes people identify negatively, as when a manager overidentifies with his subordinates to the point where he cannot exercise authority over them. Identification is sometimes called social learning. It occurs both consciously and unconsciously.

When images of other people become fixed or internalized we call it *introjection.* The superego, representing the voices of the parents and other powerful figures, is an introject. Sometimes we even introject destructive self-images, as, for example, when a successful, powerful manager now in middle age still sees himself in his unconscious mind's eye as a helpless small child. The very fact that introjection means that the image is locked in indicates that negative reactions to one's own picture of oneself usually are not amenable to change by managerial means.

Sublimation is the channeling of drives into socially acceptable activities, such as play, work, hobbies, community services, and so forth, which are also in keeping with the person's capacities and values. For most people occupation is the major mode of sublimation. We choose that kind of work, however unconsciously, which helps us maintain our psychological equilibrium by combining in one pattern our preferred ways of handling drives, superego, ego competences, and the outside world. Building houses, for example, is a far more constructive way of sublimating aggression than attacking others. Helping others as a community volunteer meets one's own dependency needs by turning them into assistance to others and is far more constructive to society than denying that one has such needs. These three are character-forming or personality-building mechanisms. There is another which operates continuously: *repression*. Repression is a storing or containing mechanism. We repress or "forget" things which are psychologically painful. We also repress or hold down feelings which cause us immediate difficulty. If we cannot discharge our aggressive feelings appropriately in the form of standing up to other people, because we have been taught that to do so is not nice, we may unconsciously automatically keep such feelings down, containing them within us like steam in a boiler. If, in the process of growing up, we have tried to reach out to and love others, and these efforts have been repulsed, we may repress feelings of affection and become known as a cold person. Repression is a necessary device, but too much of it blots out much of what one should remember, and not enough leaves one struggling too much with unconscious material. When a person loses touch with reality and hears voices or believes things which are not true, the repressive barrier has been broken and the person has lost effective control over his unconscious experiences, thoughts, and fantasies.

Because our physical and psychological functioning are very highly attuned, the balance to be maintained is a delicate one. Man's tolerances are narrow. A few degrees of fever can incapacitate him. Small variations in the balance of body fluids can result in death. Variations in psychic balance can be equally threatening. The ego therefore must make use of a wide variety of temporary mechanisms to cope with various kinds of threats. All of us frequently use these mechanisms in varying degrees. Some, by now, are so commonly known that their names are part of everyday discourse.

The most common coping mechanism is *rationalization*, the process of creating reasons to justify our actions. We rationalize in order to appease our superegos. Management actions are frequently rationalized as necessary for profitability even when they may be destructive to individuals or to the environment.

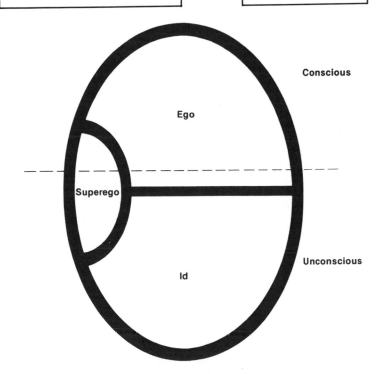

Defenses

Character Forming:
Identification
Introjection
Sublimation

Repression

Temporary:
Rationalization
Projection
Idealization
Substitution
Reaction Formation

1. Threat from Environment-Fear
   (Realistic Anxiety)
2. Threat from Superego-Guilt
   (Superego Anxiety)
3. Threat from Id-Anxiety

Conscious

Ego

Superego

Unconscious

Id

**Figure 6. Adaptational Conception II:
The Equilibrium-Maintaining Activities
of the Personality**

Poor quality or unsafe products are sometimes rationalized as "what the public wants." Decisions and actions always require some logic which frequently we have to make up, however unconsciously, if the reasons for our behavior are not clear even to us.

If accepting blame or responsibility for something is too painful for us, we can easily *project* or blame it on the next person. Historically, managements have attributed the union organization of their plants to the activities of union organizers whom they see as manipulating their workers when frequently the conditions which brought about union organization were created by managements themselves. From time to time the same has been true with respect to government regulations: the failure of industries to maintain quality control standards or professionals to control their disciplines have led to governmental intervention which is then attributed by the now regulated parties to the wish of nefarious schemers to socialize them or tell them how to run their business or profession. People who have great difficulty tolerating their own hostility, either because they can't accept the fact that they are so angry or because they can't manage that anger, frequently attribute hostility to other people. That attribution then permits them to feel justified about being hostile to those others. This is a major source of racial prejudice.

In *displacement* or *substitution,* we vent our feelings on a convenient but inappropriate target. This is the attack which follows projection. Scapegoating is just one variation of this mechanism. Managers frequently unload their disappointment in themselves onto their subordinates. Spouses and children or others who are relatively helpless are easy victims of displacement or substitution. When a man is angry at his boss, at whom he cannot strike back, it is not unusual for him to take out that anger at home.

Denial is a variant of repression. "It doesn't bother me," we say, when in reality we are very much bothered and our behavior shows it. Managers and executives, particularly those of middle age, frequently deny they have any psychological problem because they think they must solve all their problems themselves. Many people deny they have health problems, despite medical findings, by violating special diets or failing to take appropriate precautions. Some deny that they are mortal, for example by smoking cigarettes when warning labels indicate a clear danger of harm to health. Many people deny they are angry or deny the intensity of their angry feelings. This is especially true when they also have affection for or great dependency on the very people at whom they are, and feel they should not be, angry.

Reaction formation means behaving outwardly the opposite of how we feel inside: a person who is repressing great hostility may present himself to others as unaggressive, or even obsequious. People who feel helpless may go to great extremes to show how powerful they are, even to the point of devoting their lives to becoming tycoons or great political figures. A person who deep inside himself thinks he is bad may, as a consequence, present himself as a model of a good, helpful human being who seeks nothing for himself.

Idealization is overvaluing another, as happens when falling in love, or promoting someone because he does *one* part of his job well, conveniently ignoring the fact that he does not do all of it well. Idealization creates the most frequent mistakes in selecting and placing people because it interferes with seeing their behavior accurately.

Overcontrol of feelings leads to a constant state of emergency, or anxiety about the possibility that the feelings will escape. This, in turn, requires continued defensiveness. When the body reacts repeatedly to psychological emergencies, physical wear and tear or psychophysiological illness is the inevitable result. Much hypertension, coronary disease, ulcers, and other illnesses have their origin in, or are compounded by, psychological stress.

A person has essentially four ways of coping with his drives: (1) channeling them into problem-solving or environment-mastering activity; (2) displacing them onto substitute targets; (3) containing or holding on to them by repression; (4) turning them against himself, which leads to self-defeating behavior, accidents, and, in extreme form, suicide. We all use all of these modes in varying degrees much of the time. The problem is in overusing the less constructive ways of utilizing energies for

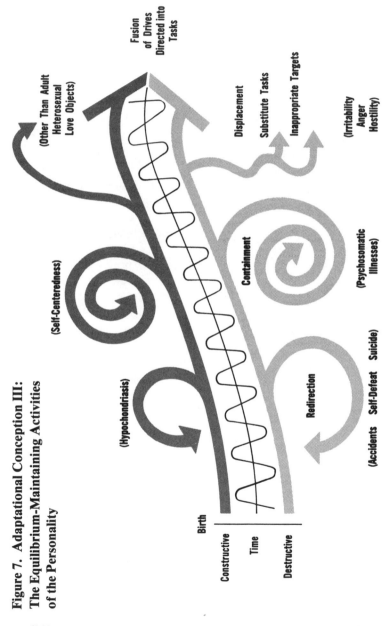

Figure 7. Adaptational Conception III:
The Equilibrium-Maintaining Activities
of the Personality

[38]

personal and social enhancement. The task for the executive is to create ways of directing energies into common tasks or problem solving rather than into defensiveness.

A person's favorite defense mechanisms become part of his mode of adapting to the world. They become evident to others as his dominant personality traits. Some people are blandly unconcerned about all of the threats and tragedies which may exist around them (denial). Others see themselves surrounded by a hostile world (projection). Each sees the world only as his or her traits and defenses permit him. For some, the world is made up of kind and friendly people and there is much to learn and do. For others, the world is comprised of people who are hostile and unfriendly and nothing new or stimulating or adventuresome ever happens. By the use of his defenses, as well as his capacities, each person actively shapes his world; he is not merely shaped by it as if he were a malleable blob of clay.

Our task will be to explain and discuss these processes in greater detail by translating them into their implications for problems of supervision, leadership, managerial processes, and organizational structure. The theory is extremely complex. You cannot expect to be able to know it and handle it with great familiarity from this cursory outline any more than you could take a brief course on atomic physics and be an atomic physicist. However, we can help create a frame of reference out of this theory and experiences with it which may contribute to a greater understanding of the problems with which you will have to deal.

Summary

It is important to emphasize again that feelings are the most powerful human motivators. A person's feeling about himself, and particularly how well one feels he or she is meeting the demands of the ego ideal, is the most crucial of all. The wise executive will understand that self-motivation is to be cherished and nurtured. His role is to do just that.

When people can meet the demands of their ego ideals, they feel pleasure in functioning, or in activity for its own sake. Robert W. White calls this *efficacy,* or a feeling of doing something, of being active or effective, of having an influence on

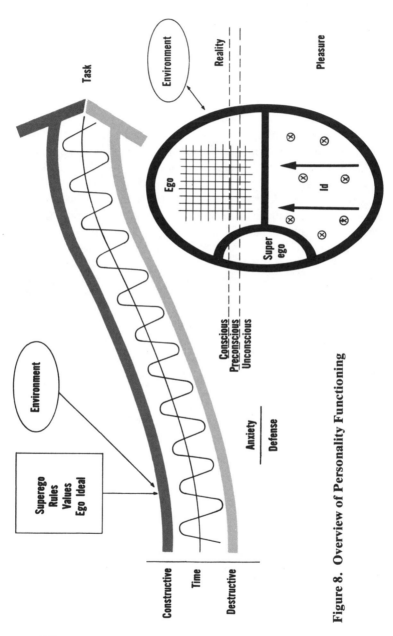

Figure 8. Overview of Personality Functioning

something.[5] People need activity to stay in touch with the world outside themselves and to feel competent in mastering it. Activity for its own sake is a major aspect of the adaptive process, he notes, and a vital theme in the growth of personality. Competence is the cumulative result of the whole history of transactions that lead to feelings of efficacy. The feeling of being able to have some effect on people, to get them to listen, of being able to provide for ourselves, to do some of the things we want, to receive and give some of the love and help we want—this feeling of social competence is the foundation stone of self-respect and security.

Work is a major activity through which a person establishes his or her competence and thereby meets lifelong multiple psychological needs and unfolding personality patterns. The executive, as a manager of organizations and a leader of people, is inevitably an instrument for psychological good or harm for many people. When he or she manages an organization psychologically well, it is more effective as an organization and healthy for the people in it; when he or she manages it psychologically poorly, its capacity for adaptation and perpetuation is undermined, and the organization is destructive to the people who comprise it. It is precisely these issues which make human behavior in organizations fundamental to the managerial role.

Chapter 2

Emotional Stress

Emotional stress or mental illness begins when the balancing forces of the personality are not functioning properly. During any period of emotional distress, a person may be said to be temporarily mentally ill. This may occur either because the threats or emergencies are continuous and the defensive mechanisms must be overused, or because for some reason the executive forces of the personality are overcome or impaired. When a person is drunk his behavior certainly differs from that of his more sober moments. A person under the influence of drugs also has less control and direction over himself. These and certain physical incapacities like brain tumors or severe debilitating illness may be viewed as impairments.

Points of Vulnerability

There are two implications then: (1) Every person at one time or another, to a greater or lesser degree, is mentally ill; (2) every person has his or her breaking point. Given enough stress of a kind to which one is particularly vulnerable, anybody will break down.

Superego Conflict. Turning to the structural aspect of personality, one sees signs in organizations of frequent and intense conflict between ego and superego. This may occur when people are asked to behave in ways which violate their own internal standards, as, for example, in producing shoddy products or misrepresenting goods and services or carrying out company policies and practices inimical to others. The guilt which results is readily evident. We have seen examples of it with respect to the leaks of government information. There are many other commonplace examples in criticisms of the advertising industry and of high-pressure tactics in the sale of retirement homes. Less evident, but no less pressing, is the guilt which arises when the gap increases between the ego ideal and the self-image. The gap can be increased as a result of organizational practices on the one hand, and personal change on the other.

The self-image, and therefore self-esteem, is lowered when people feel manipulated by forces beyond their control, when they feel themselves to be demeaned or their work role is demeaning, when they are pitted against each other and are compelled to identify themselves as losers, when they are victimized by organizational policies and practices, and when they view themselves as manipulators or exploiters of others. Arbitrary managerial decisions, much of so-called management by objectives, most organization practices related to promotion and compensation, and many of the job demands created by mechanistic systems of industrial engineering and accounting contribute to such feelings. In particular, the inability to view themselves as valued members of organizations contributing significantly to the resolution of problems which confront the organization is a major source of lowered self-esteem in contemporary organizations of all kinds.

Guilt is always engendered when people are asked to evaluate or appraise others and experience those practices as being destructive because unconsciously to be critical of someone else is the same as to destroy the other. Similar feelings are engendered by intense rivalry, particularly in triumphing over older and more experienced persons in the organization and in having to discharge others. Similarly, guilt is experienced when people have to maneuver around organizational policies and channels in order to accomplish their tasks.

On a more personal level, the gap between the ego ideal and the self-image increases when people age and no longer feel themselves to have the same adaptive skills they had before. This is especially true in a context of intense competitive rivalry.

Drives. Malfunction or dysfunction occurs with respect to the drives when the two become defused, when the constructive energies of the personality, derived from the sexual drive, no longer adequately temper the aggressive drive. The aggression is thereupon diverted from effective utilization in problem-solving activities. Such defusion may occur in response to excessive external stimuli which provoke anger. It may also occur regularly in people who are chronically angry and who therefore vent their anger onto others. Thus, scapegoating, sadistic behavior, overcontrolling behavior, absenteeism, accidents, sabotage, resistance, and internal strife are common incidents in most organizations.

It is difficult for many people to express affection, support and approval—sometimes because of their own personalities, and sometimes because organizational norms do not encourage such behavior or organizational pressures militate against it. This deprives their subordinates of the infusion they need to sustain the dominance of their own constructive energy. Anger in one form or another then erupts. Frequently persons in authoritative roles say, "I'm not going to hold people's hands," or, "They come to work and they go home, and that's all there is to it. That's what work is for." Thus, anger can be provoked by executives, managers, and supervisors who are unwilling or unable to provide adequate support and direction to others or help subordinates resolve their organizational and interpersonal problems.

Defusion occurs when people are unable to adequately control their impulses, either because these impulses are too powerful and therefore overwhelm them or because organizational pressures precipitate outbursts. Unrelenting pressure for productivity, inability or unwillingness to solve frustrating problems, or simple inefficiency are typical precipitants. Inadequate or incorrect information, which leads to feelings of unworthiness or threat, is another. Undue emphasis on organizational "family" relationships or paternalistic demands for loyalty may deflect the constructive drive from tasks to be accomplished and conflicts to be resolved and thereby exacerbate guilt.

Dysfunction occurs also when there are inadequate or inappropriate channels for the *constructive* expression of aggression, that is, when people can't get at—let alone resolve—problems inherent in the work situation. This is seen in extreme cases when people attack each other, as in intra-organizational struggles, or when they destroy their own property, as in race riots.

Obsolescence. The aging process and occupational obsolescence both contribute to the decreased capacity of the ego to adapt. In adult life aging means gradual physical and mental deterioration. Though the pace at which these processes occur may differ among persons, nevertheless, as a person's capacities decline, he or she must become more dependent on others. Ultimately those who live to an advanced age will have to be cared for. This physical and mental decline serves to lower the self-image. People knew themselves to be more adequate and more capable. They were often held in higher esteem and were more directly influential in their own lives and the activities around them. This lowered self-image is depressed even further in a culture which depreciates age and values youth. The depreciation process is accelerated by the increase in medical problems, greater loneliness, and inadequate Social Security and other protection provisions which lead people who are already aged to feel they are abandoned and frightens those who are moving toward their older years.

The aging process begins to have its effects on people in managerial ranks quite early. Managers in their thirties begin to be concerned that younger competitors fresh from business schools will have more knowledge and energy than they have. These fears accelerate as middle age approaches and, increasingly, younger people are sought for competitive jobs requiring greater imagination. For younger managers, age is a milepost of advancement. Many pace their career movement in such a way as to feel defeated if they do not move upward in the hierarchy as rapidly as their passing years indicate they should. Feelings of defeat begin to be followed by depression, which in turn decreases the capacity of the ego to adapt.

It is true that as people age they tend to become less imaginative and to retain the ways of coping which have been effective for them in the past. If they have evolved successful managerial modes, these will be repeated just as an artist as he ages repeats a characteristic style in his canvases. To the extent to which a person is inflexible in his modes of coping, he or she becomes more restricted, and obsolete, as aging proceeds.

The lowered self-image resulting from the aging process, unless supported by various forms of achievement which meet the demands of the ego ideal, tends to make it harder to learn new skills which would restore the self-image. A lowered self-image makes mistakes more intolerable. If mistakes are intolerable, learning becomes threatening because no one can learn without making mistakes.

Occupational obsolescence goes hand in glove with the aging process. Not only is it difficult to keep up with advancing information, new techniques, and changes in market demand within a given skill, trade or discipline, but also it is hard for people to cope with the fact that even highly refined skills may come to have no commercial value at all. There is certainly considerably less use for bricklayers with increased use of modular units and glass walls. Computers have made obsolete many activities previously done by hand or by slower methods. Even highly refined engineering skills, necessary for the development of space vehicles, may have no parallel use in a civilian economy.

Having developed competence, an ego function, and an occupational or professional self-image built on that competence, those whose competence is less valued have lowered self-images. Still trying to preserve those self-images, many find it difficult to retrain themselves in other occupations or in other skills. They are subject to long periods of unemployment followed by new jobs which usually are at lower pay and demand less skill than their previous work. They continue to have to live with decreased self-images, feelings of disappointment in and anger with themselves. They act as if what has happened to them is somehow quite unfair because unconsciously they have been following a script which said that if they did what they did, they could view themselves as competent. They did it and discovered to their dismay that they cannot. A combination of aging and obsolescence makes people less desirable in the occupational marketplace, in turn making them feel less valued. Think, for example, of the machinist who can no longer see as well as he used to but who must run lathes at closer tolerances, or aircraft controllers whose reaction time is slowed by age but who must now guide jet aircraft requiring split-second responses. Those over forty years of age have an increasingly difficult time reestablishing themselves when, because of age or obsolescence or other forces, they have lost their jobs. The difficulty of finding a new job multiplies with each advancing year.

When people who have become too specialized or are no longer technically up-to-date feel themselves to be less adequate, they are therefore more readily threatened by any environmental circumstance. If in the course of aging or moving from place to place they lose contact with valued friends and associates, or are unable to use favored modes of behavior, or are deprived of environmental support or of leaders whom they had trusted, they commonly experience loss which is followed by anger with self and others and frequently depression. Merger, retirement, transfer, promotion, all carry with them the pains of such losses despite whatever gains may result.

Change of any kind necessarily means uprooting or severing. By definition, to uproot is to lose contact with one's sources of nourishment and anchorage. To sever is to cut off one's ties, also to lose anchorage. Both images reflect feelings of deprivation, instability, and indeed even the threat of potential death. Uprooting and severing experiences make people feel that they are more alone in coping with the complexities of a threatening environment. People become more constricted, more guarded, more rigid, and more stereotyped in their reactions as they devote more energy to maintaining their equilibrium in the face of such losses.

Most people assume that minor losses are of no significance

and that even major ones can be made up. To a certain extent those conclusions are valid. However, as I shall show later, loss experiences are more psychologically and physiologically costly than most people are aware. The feelings associated with them tend to be masked by our protective efforts to cover over the pain we experience.

The ego allows us to integrate memory images of people, ways of accomplishing skills, favorite geographical locations, or personal items—all those things we hold dear as part of our way of life. When integration is disrupted by change, we are compelled to reorganize a new network or configuration from which we can draw psychological nourishment and sustenance.

This need to create a new configuration of anchor points for social stability and adaptation to the job and the organization, as well as to find new avenues of gratification, requires considerable personal investment. Psychologically we race our motors in an effort to recover our personal momentum. This personal psychological task becomes more difficult in new situations because the ego is futher beleaguered due to the new demands being made on it. For example, when historically highly controlled organizations must become more decentralized, when previously authoritarian managers are asked to become more democratic, when dependent employees are required to become more aggressive, not only have they lost support, gratifications, and goals, but also they must cope with new requirements for which they may be unprepared or unsuited.

The ego may have difficulty in adapting because the person does not get adequate information from peers. Without that information the person may not know what to do or how to do it or what is coming next. Rumors replace facts. Reality is ambiguous. Organizational structures may be inchoate or unstable. Key figures may no longer be present; panic ensues. The ego is at a loss to maintain its equilibrium. Loss and demand are the twin forces which, operating simultaneously, stretch the adaptive capacity of the ego. One never occurs without the other. The two comprise a psychological tax which we implicitly recognize when we use the word "overtaxed" and speak of "nervous exhaustion."

Contractual Violation. Another threat to the ego, because it lowers self-image and increases anxiety, is the loss of the context for the ego's equilibrium-maintaining activities. People unconsciously select organizations and kinds of work largely on the basis of an unconscious psychological contract. That is, people choose organizations and work which fit their unconscious needs for managing their drives, the demands of their superegos, including the ego ideal, and the use of their skills and capacities. There is a configurational pattern of feelings, thoughts, and behavior which we call personality. The person either fits his to a matching configurational pattern in an organization or adapts part of that organization to match his pattern. There is, for example, a different personality configuration among people who seek managerial roles in AT&T as contrasted with their counterparts in IBM. Both in turn differ significantly from those who are managers for Sears, Roebuck. These differences are readily recognizable by anyone who has contact with all three groups, or other similar groups. Each company has its characteristic way of doing business and its characteristic organization structure. People who remain in those organizations are likely to do so because they are comfortable with both. Employees frequently unconsciously view their employing organization as being maternal or paternal.[6] A good fit between organization and person means not only having an opportunity to use one's skills but also finding a congenial situation for the practice of one's values, or the expression of his preferred modes of handling drives and of relating to people. Organizations, therefore, become supportive contexts, and work becomes a medium for maintaining the psychological equilibrium by fulfilling the unconscious psychological contract.[7]

Organic Change. Physiological impairment is another way in which the ego's adaptive ability is weakened. In some organizations this poses a difficult and dangerous problem. For example, some years ago following a series of train accidents, the medical director of a well-known railroad was concerned about screening engineers who might be accident-prone. Questioning disclosed that most men did not become engineers until they were at least fifty-five years old, at which time there were beginning to be organic brain changes in some. Many in their seventies were still operating trains. These men were examined annually by their own physicians. None was required to have a neurological examination. As it turned out, some were operating their engines at seventy miles per hour in thirty-five mile-per-hour zones, no longer able to see or react to the speed limit signs quickly enough, and accidents would result.

Ego Development. The ego's adaptive processes can also be inhibited by inadequate developmental experiences. This is one of the problems now facing organizations as they employ increasing numbers of people who have been educationally, culturally, and perhaps psychologically disadvantaged.

By inadequate developmental experiences we generally mean that the person has missed out on or has not been able to master certain basic skills and competences which are necessary building blocks in the formation of an array of modes of coping with the average expectable environment with which an adult must deal in that culture. For example, many children suffer from an inability to read at a level commensurate with adult requirements. In part this occurs because of lack of a stimulus to read from the parent, in part because of the scarcity of reading materials, in part because of poor teaching, and sometimes because of physical or emotional handicaps. As mentioned earlier, impairment in the identification process may make it difficult to emulate a well-defined role model. A culture with a heavy emphasis on intrafamily ties at the expense of experiences outside the family, one which decries mixing with those who do not share the same religion or tradition, may make it difficult for young people to learn to interact with others who are different from themselves. An overprotective family which denies its children the opportunity to acquire work skills may deny them the opportunity to do for themselves what adults should be able to do. Children who do not learn to play early on have difficulty subsequently interacting with others on a recreational level. Those who have been discriminated against and denied certain maturing experiences, like access to social activities or facilities or educational resources, may as a consequence have gaps in their developmental experiences.

As a result when people who are thus handicapped in one way or another go to work, they may have to learn as part of their orientation and training process not only the skills required for a given job but perhaps even more basic reading and writing skills, reasoning skills, social skills, and standards of performance.

Ego development will vary from culture to culture. A highly intelligent middle-class white American male probably would have considerable difficulty surviving in an environment which a semiliterate Eskimo has mastered by developing understanding and knowledge as he grows up that become his intuition and skills as an adult. With sufficient teaching, coaching, and protective guidance, the American might acquire enough of these skills to survive. But without that help he may well die. So it is with those who experience severe deprivation then come into the work force.

Age-Appropriate Activities. Still another aspect of adaptation which is only now beginning to be touched upon is that of age-appropriate activities. Adult life, according to Erikson's conceptualization, mentioned earlier, is divided into three stages. The first stage, that of intimacy, is also the period when a person establishes himself in his career, acquires the skills of that career, and is most vigorous in his potentially novel attack on the problems of that career period. This is followed by the stage of generativity, or middle age, when there is heavy concentration on the development of others while simultaneously renewing one's own goals and values, and finally by the period beyond fifty-five, the stage of integrity, or completion, in which one integrates his life experience with the demands of his ego ideal. There is as yet no adequate differentiation in organizations among people of these respective age groups with respect to the kinds of work which are most suitable for one or another stage. It is irrational to expect most middle-aged people to approach a task with the same kind of innovative flair as younger people, yet frequently that is what is expected when competition is placed on a simplistic plane. The psychological inability to meet the requirements of a given task because of one's life stage is a source of great stress. The ego is expected to meet demands with which it can no longer cope or which are unrelated to its stage of development.

Role Conflict and Ambiguity. A primary problem for the ego in its adaptation in an organizational structure, or even with respect to independent professional activity, is its inability to meet the demands of the ego ideal. People's role ambiguity, being uncertain about what they are supposed to do or how well they are doing it, reduces their ability to act competently.[8] Given the severity of most people's superegos and the consequent tendency to be hypercritical of themselves, in the absence of information to the contrary, people quickly jump to self-criticism, which in turn leads to the lowered self-image, which in turn leads to forms of defensive behavior that frequently are counterproductive. Furthermore, they run the risk of external criticism of their performance, which in turn will lower the self-image. It is a commonplace that when most people in organizations are asked, "How do you know where you stand?" they respond, "By the squawk index." This means that most people perennially operate from a defensive position, ready to be criticized and threatened with lowered self-image. They see themselves as always vulnerable to loss of self-esteem and potentially unable to meet the internalized ego ideal, which involves considerations of being good, doing well, and demonstrating competence.

Given the harshness of the superego—and the more competent people are, the more self demanding they are, and therefore the more prone to be self-critical—superior-subordinate relationships become particularly important. I have often asked executive groups the question, "How do you know how you are doing?" In response they will usually report the statistics of performance, feedback from peers, subordinates, appraisals, and other criteria. I then ask, "Suppose that you know by your own internal standards that you've done a good job, and your boss doesn't say anything, what do you do?" For a moment the executives deny that the boss's reaction has much meaning. But then, typically, they delineate a sequence of behavior that would be likely to follow. They would first try to call his attention to what they have done. If he did not respond, then they would work harder to try to prove themselves. If the boss still did not respond, they would try to talk with him. If he were still noncommittal in conversation, then their anger would mount. They would then very likely take an extra drink and displace some of their hostility onto their children or their subordinates. Then they would begin to withdraw from their work, getting by with minimal effort. Finally, they would ultimately quit.

The Need for Confirmation. The point is that despite all of the presumed objective criteria of performance, the crucial variable which recurs repetitively is the need for confirmation (approval) from superiors. Approval both enhances the self-image and gives permission for behavior, so that people need not fear being criticized for usurping the role of higher authority.

In the studies of role stress, the crucial role senders are the superiors. In a more recent study of role ambiguity, the same crucial experience of superior-subordinate relationship arises. Some theorists ignore relationships with superiors. Others deny their importance. From my point of view, they are more powerful than either subordinate or superior usually recognizes.

In recent years there has been a tendency to put heavy emphasis on group approval or peer approval at the expense of the approval of superiors. In part this stems from the current cultural emphasis on the importance of peers in adolescence and early adulthood. However, in my judgment this emphasis is considerably misplaced. Young people are always reacting to their feelings about their parents despite what they may say. Clinical experience demonstrates a very powerful need for approval from parents. Though many people may deny it, the same pressures hold with respect to their wish to be well regarded and held in esteem by those who employ them or supervise them. When superiors fail to understand this, subordinates feel on the one hand unappreciated, and on the other as if they are walking on psychological eggs. In the great hue and cry for participative management, many managers, failing to understand this phenomenon, have abandoned decision-making to subordinates, who are then paralyzed into inactivity because, while they may have been given oral permission, they feel that they do not have the psychological permission. They have heard the words that promise that they are free to act but do not have the reinforcement of repeated affirmation or supportive behavior.

There are two reasons why this phenomenon is so powerful. The first is the power differential between parents and children. Parents have great power over their children in the earliest and most impressionable years. Children view their own competence vis-à-vis that of the parents as extremely limited, and, being dependent on the parents, they feel quite powerless. Furthermore, given the oedipal experience and the feelings stirred up by it, frequently they feel they have no right to act in the parental role without the reinforced consent of the parent. People who are promoted usually have to contend with such feelings, even with the formal permission of promotion. Others may need to test whether they have approval in order to reassure themselves, particularly when such issues as aging and obsolescence intervene.

The second reason that the power of the superior is so important is that it is magnified in the eyes of the subordinate by transference. Transference is a concept which refers to the fact that people unconsciously bring into present situations attitudes derived from childhood experiences. There is a powerful tendency to attribute to superiors at work some of the same qualities that people experience in their relationships to their parents. Some people therefore act in a meek and submissive way, expecting to be criticized and attacked by the superior, some in an arrogant and demanding way, as if a good offense is the best defense, and some in a recalcitrant way, as if recapitulating the stubbornness of childhood. Thus, employees unconsciously will tend to bring into work situations some of the same expectations of power figures—superiors—that they had of their own parents. This means that the superior-subordinate relationships take on even more significant psychological proportions than most people assume.

Organizational Structure and Practice

Some people assume that emotional stress is solely a matter of individual susceptibility. However, although individual vulnerabilities may vary, from what we have already discussed it should be apparent that everyone is likely to be affected by the manner in which work practices are organized and carried out.

Pyramidal Structure and Defeat. Organizational structure and organizational practices also relate to people's self-images and ego ideals. For example, although much is said about organizations as instruments of achievement for individuals, and motivational practices as being more rewarding than punishing, the fact is that bureaucratic organizations essentially are geared for defeat. That is, for each person who is promoted a number are left behind.

Given an organizational value system which emphasizes managerial achievement, such a practice leaves behind many "career people" who are angry with themselves and their organizations because they have been passed over. In essence they are told, "You are nothing. You have had it. You are a defeated one." The consequence is considerable chronic repressed anger in many organizations. Laurence Peter has made a universal joke out of the "Peter Principle," the notion that people rise to their level of incompetence.[9] Yet I am sure that many people become incompetent because they are made so by the underlying depression which paralyzes their activities after they had been defined as defeated, as failures. This phenomenon is made even worse by the intense pressure toward early retirement, which is essentially a castration of mature people who have had little opportunity and less support to adapt to rapidly changing economic circumstances. As a consequence, they see themselves as utter failures. Executives in such a position frequently ask the question uncomprehendingly, "What did I do wrong?"

These experiences of human defeat, of male by male, have great significance because they are part of a biological pattern. There is a long history of animal studies which indicates that animals lower in the pecking order within a given flock, pack, or other unit have a significantly higher incidence of death and withdrawal than do victors.[10] Defeated male mice cling to the corners of their cages for their bodily functions as contrasted to the victors, who may extrude body products anywhere in their cages.[11]

Defeated male cockroaches die at significantly higher rates than those who are victorious.[12] Among men, there is an inverse relationship between position in the hierarchy of the organization and the incidence and prevalence of both physical and mental illness.[13] We do not yet have sufficient data on women in managerial roles.

Object Attachments. When the ego cannot meet the pressures of the id, to which I referred earlier, it has yet another adaptive difficulty. The ego needs avenues for discharge of drives or feelings derived from them. When it loses objects of affection and thereby sources for the return of affection, the ego experiences deprivation, loss, and helplessness. Disappointment and anger follow.

When sources of support and affection are gone, when people's networks of relationships by which they have accomplished their work are disrupted by management actions which pit people against each other instead of letting them work together, then depressions result. When there is no time for managers to support people, or when the span of control is so wide that people who need support no longer have it, then again depression follows.

All of these losses are captured in the characteristic failure story in management, the good salesman who is promoted to become a poor sales manager. A good salesman characteristically devotes himself to pleasing his customers. From serving them and being in continuous contact with them, he receives signals of approval, he is held in esteem, he is continually patted. When such a person is made sales manager, he shuffles papers. He loses the avenues for support and affection which previously were so important to him and in turn he is unable to support the salesmen who report to him because he needs so much affection himself. Such problems occur in many different forms at almost all levels in organizations.

Overstimulation. There are also difficulties in adaptation when there is stimulation of the drives beyond what people can handle. Psychologists and psychiatrists who served in the military forces know of the sexual stimulation brought about merely by proximity to others which frequently results in homosexual panic. Such panic reactions have also occurred in encounter groups and in similar training activities frequently undertaken naively by managements. It occurs also when there is invasion of already well-defined unisexual groups, as, for example, when young and pretty telephone operators are introduced into a group of maiden lady operators. Such problems are likely to escape the notice of characteristic sociological and socio-psychological studies unless there is a thorough understanding of personality variables.

A more commonplace experience of overstimulation is that which has to do with the management of aggression. Frequently people who work face-to-face with irate customers, such as airlines service representatives, retail clerks, and others subject to attack, have great difficulty managing their own hostile reactions. Policemen typically have frequent provocation to anger and aggression. On the other hand, those who come in close proximity to others of the opposite sex may find themselves sexually aroused. It is for that reason that the Hippocratic oath prohibits sexual relationships with patients and why there are powerful codes of ethics governing the relationships of various kinds of therapists with their clients or patients.

Overstimulation of aggression can occur under experiences of great frustration, and overstimulation of needs for affection in times of tragedy, sorrow, or misfortune. In such instances people may well act in ways that are quite different from their ordinary modes of behavior.

There are, then, stimulations which can make for adaptive difficulties on the part of the ego, when it is unable to meet the pressures of the id. It is for these reasons that in times of stress there is need for closer, more frequent supervision, for greater opportunity to talk about the stress experiences and to evolve modes of coping with them, and for protecting people against temporary vulnerability. A good example of an effort to do all three is the labor-management negotiation activity in some industries prior to the end of a contract. Both unions and management know that a strike stimulates hostility in which both people and property are likely to get hurt. It is therefore far wiser for people to argue their way into an agreement long before the contract ends than to become militantly hostile after that time.

Neurotic Conflict. In addition, there are focal problems for the ego which stem from id conflicts. These are seen in classical failures like the man who, promoted to a vice-presidency, jumps from an eighteenth-story window on the first day of his tenure. Frequently one sees an executive who does well in his upward climb until he moves beyond his father's level. When it becomes clear to him, however unconsciously, that he has exceeded (in the primitive part of his mind that means defeated) his father, he fails. Neither he nor those around him are likely to understand why a man who has been highly successful suddenly fails. These become organizational problems because insufficient attention is given to complex personality factors in most executive selection processes. Sometimes organizations unwittingly facilitate managerial self-defeat and self-destruction.

In recent years we have seen the same phenomenon in major political figures who could not move into adequate managerial roles because of the psychological significance to them of being in these roles. Some cannot accept and manage their own aggressive impulses, for to express aggression in the form of assuming a leadership role, in which one has to give direction to others, to manipulate political forces, and to act on (as contrasted with talking about) what one believes, presents them with a conflict which they can resolve only by rejecting the leadership role.

This same phenomenon, the inability to accept and utilize one's own impulses, particularly aggressive ones, plagues certain kinds of organizations such as hospitals, church institutions, educational institutions, and the like. People who choose work which takes them into such institutions usually do so in part out of the need to deny more open expression of aggression in the form of competitive effort or exercising power over others. For example, if one asks students in a graduate school of business why they are there they will speak quite freely of their wish for power and achievement, money and position. They have few problems in identifying themselves as aggressive-competitive people. However, when one asks the same question of people in schools of hospital, educational, or public administration, the response will usually be in terms of contribution to the public good, which frequently masks and rationalizes the unconscious wish for power. As a result, the underlying aggression, unacceptable in consciousness, will tend to be managed in a more clandestine fashion by manipulation behind the scenes. Consequently, it is much more difficult in such institutions to know what is going on, and there is frequent complaint of dirty politics. These issues frequently pass for role conflict.

Rivalry. There are special stresses of occupation related to development which have gone largely unrecognized. Among them is the classical problem of intense rivalry with a parent, which stems from the oedipal period. This is seen most vividly among entrepreneurs.

Characteristically entrepreneurs have had great unresolved oedipal struggles with their fathers and as a result cannot accept supervision from other men. Given this kind of conflict, typically they cannot tolerate rivalry. As a result they exploit their organizations. They tend to "marry the organization" and to use the organization as if it were a mistress and simultaneously their means of identification and their "baby." They tend to engage in internecine warfare with up-and-coming people in their own organizations and immediately cut down anyone who seeks to rise to a position of power and who thereby threatens to take their organization away from them.

Consequently, such organizations have great difficulty in adapting as their progenitors age and are unable to change with changes in the environment. The organizations become obsolete. People in them run great job risk and many are suppressed in their jobs. When such a leader either retires or leaves his organization, he usually leaves behind a highly dependent group of people who now suffer from the loss of a charismatic leader and are left with a maladaptive organization. This is a source of great stress which becomes even more severe when, following his demise, there is exacerbated rivalry for a position of power, or the organization is merged with another, or simply falls apart. Ultimately, since organizations are such an important component of society, we will probably see the day when organizations abused in this way by their founders will be taken from them, just as children are rescued by agencies of society when they are abused by their parents.

A subset of this problem is the intensity of conflict in family businesses. There are nearly a million family businesses in the United States. They are more common in other countries. The intensity of rivalry and the exacerbation of conflict and guilt in such businesses is more severe than in nonfamily businesses. This is a source of stress about which there is as yet little information and even fewer ways of helping people to cope.

Developmental Issues. Some of the difficulties which arise from developmental issues have to do with the misplacement of people in roles which are more adequate to persons in another developmental life stage. I have already referred to placing middle-aged managers in competitive tasks more appropriate to younger persons. We might also view the same issue from the obverse point of view: frequently young people are asked merely to wait in line for their managerial places and promised the opportunity to act in their later years, a time more conducive to reflection than to action. In increasing numbers, managers and executives are confronting multiple careers, mid-career changes, middle-age crises, and the trauma associated with retirement. In addition, certain occupations are specifically related to life stages and are marked by transitional difficulties. Professional athletes notoriously must deal with this problem. Scientists, creative artists, aircraft controllers, and many others frequently find themselves in occupational stress situations related to the specific life stages.

One of the major tasks of managers and executives is to train their own replacements, and an important concern in business organizations therefore is management development. But it is difficult to get people from 21 to 35 to be concerned about developing other people. They are at that stage in their own lives when they are necessarily preoccupied with their own careers. That period is a self-centered one. It is too intimately bound up with developing a network of adult relationships and in the generation of new families to allow sufficient psychological energy for the development of others, which might mean contributing to the development of potential rivals. On the other hand, it is equally irrational to expect a man of fifty-four to operate at the same level of intensity as a man of twenty-five in the same occupation. Such a person who already has established himself might do far better in the development of others where he can bring to bear his wisdom and experience, integrated with his need to maintain a contributing but less competitive role than he had before. Finally, the tasks of reorganizing, or integrating the prospective future with the momentum of the past, are the tasks of older people, those fifty-five and older.

There is much research to be done on differentiating tasks psychologically with respect to ages and stages of development and to delineating the developmental periods in adult life so that a better fit can be evolved for people and jobs. When we can do so, we can prevent much occupational stress. By the same token we will know better how to relieve stress arising from such psychological binds.

Fixation and Regression. Stress can arise either from fixation at a given level of development or from a regression to a previous level of development. People whose occupational choice appears to be significantly related to a stage of personality development are likely to behave in ways typical of that stage. They are likely, under occupational stress, to have symptoms indicative of a regression to a more primitive form of that stage of development. This is seen most clearly in those people whose personalities have strong residual elements from the oral and anal stages of psychosexual development. For example, those in advertising, acting, editing, and other occupational roles which have an important oral component (a stage when dependency needs are most powerful) seem to have greater difficulty in managerial roles which require them to take charge of a situation and to act aggressively. It is not without reason that a major symptom among people in the newspaper business is alcoholism. That symptom has as its characteristics a bottle and total dependency when drunk.

Conversely, a person whose occupational choice is more firmly anchored in the anal stage of development and who is a tightly organized, compulsive person is more likely to have difficulty when, for example, as an executive vice president of a consumer products company he must deal with media people on advertising, promotion, creative art, and other more oral activities requiring greater flexibility and looseness. Such a person has great difficulty letting go. He cannot tolerate the fantasy life of more creative people, their difficulty in maintaining schedules, and their inability to respond to tight organizational control. Similarly, a man in his mid-fifties whose forte is systems is likely to have great difficulty coping with rapidly changing styles which are the stock in trade of a department store. He will also find it difficult to supervise younger people in their early twenties who are in touch with the moods of that age period and who themselves exhibit some of the sensitivity to flair and buying and selling which are the essence of profitability in such a business.

Character Flexibility. Between the lines of this discussion so far, I have talked about adaptation. I have viewed occupation as a mode of coping with the equilibrium-maintaining activities of the personality and stresses as dysfunctions or malfunctions in the capacity to maintain an effective adaptation level.

However, some forms of maladaptive behavior are adaptive in particular circumstances. There is, for example, the rigidity of certain kinds of people, which, though useful up to a certain point in time or certain stage in their occupational development, then becomes dysfunctional. Characteristically dependent or rigid people who may do well in highly formalized, controlled organizations begin to lose out when they move into higher-level responsibilities requiring greater initiative and more flexibility, or when such organizations are required to become more flexible as a result of increasingly differentiated market circumstances. This has happened in recent years in banks, petroleum companies, insurance companies, large retail organizations, and even in many manufacturing organizations. The adaptational problems of such people become very severe. There are few guidelines in the organizational behavior literature for organizational leadership to evolve transitions with minimal trauma.

Similarly, some men and women seek executive positions as a

reaction formation against an unconscious feeling of helplessness. This compensatory effort to acquire power leads such people into overcontrol which stimulates rebellion, intensifies rivalry, and paralyzes initiative. Such people can be successful until they are called upon to develop others or allow for greater initiative. If they cannot do so, they are forced into premature retirement or out of their positions of responsibility, with consequent stress. They may, meanwhile, sabotage efforts to make their organizations more flexible and to involve others more directly in organizational decision-making. They frequently demoralize their organizations, exploiting and manipulating people in them for their own psychological needs.

There are four other major character problems often seen in organizational leadership. They show up because that characteristic behavior is dysfunctional for the organization or because the people with those character styles cannot respond effectively to the demands being made upon them and therefore adapt poorly to their environments. These are the problems of the mediator-leader, the narcissistic leader, the manipulative leader, and the paranoid leader.

The mediator-leader is a person who characteristically has dealt with conflict among others by being the go-between or the trusted third party. In his own role he is frequently willing to compromise, sometimes beyond an optimum point. He funnels his aggression into problem-solving mediation but cannot himself make decisions or solve problems. Such a person as a leader paralyzes action and produces great anger and resentment among people who need guidance and direction as well as permission to act.

The narcissistic character is a highly self-centered leader whose managerial role serves largely for his personal aggrandizement. More often than not he has more than one grandly elaborate office with imposing furniture and accouterments beyond those required for his task, certainly inordinately beyond those of others in the organization. For such a person the organization serves as a claque or a self-created medium of self-approval and self-applause. Other people have little or no meaning for him.

The manipulative leader exploits people to their disadvantage, often merely to exhibit his own power. He revels in playing people off against each other. He glories both in his manipulative skill and his presumed omnipotence. Sometimes his manipulation is masked by paternalism: only he knows what is best for people, and he makes it happen to them. In a leadership role, he uses the organization merely as a manipulative instrument, and the people in it are merely his patsies. Usually the judgment of such a leader is poor.

The paranoid leader frequently is in pursuit of a hostile environment, made up of many enemies whom he must defeat. He is usually on the attack, both righteous and indignant, leading a tightly organized, intensely driven organization. He is the stuff of which heroes are made.

Military and political models might help illustrate. General Dwight D. Eisenhower would come close to being an example of the mediator-leader; General Douglas MacArthur, the narcissistic leader; Hitler, the manipulative leader; and General George Patton, the paranoid leader. These types are not pure; obviously they overlap.

Leaders like these have devastating effects on the people who must work under them. Eisenhower was successful in the military where there was staff work and decisions automatically followed; he was less so at Columbia University and as president of the United States. MacArthur's grandiosity made him think he was more powerful than the president of the United States; he was not noted for his sensitivity to the conditions under which his men worked and fought. Hitler manipulated a nation into assenting to a devastating war and the murder of millions. Patton pushed his men beyond their capacity and finally had to be removed from his command position. Such problems have long been known clinically, but they are seldom examined from the point of view of understanding them in an organizational context in order to prevent destructiveness to people and organizations and to alleviate the potential stress.

One of the implications of this discussion is that it is imperative to assess what psychological purposes are being served when a person seeks a leadership role and at what point and under what circumstances those unconscious purposes will come into conflict with the needs of the organization and the people whom he proposes to lead. How much stress would he cause as a consequence of his own characteristic mode of adaptation? Can the organization afford that?

Threats to Adaptation. Another dimension of adaptive effort has to do with the psychological contract. As indicated earlier, people seek occupations and organizations which fit their psychological needs and support their equilibrium-maintaining efforts. There is, therefore, an unconscious psychological contract between the person and the organization, usually recognized only when people become disappointed at what has happened to them. As a consequence, increasingly we will see pressures toward unionization and forms of control over managements. These pressures will be efforts to force managements to make up in money and security provisions for having failed to recognize, or for having violated, the psychological contracts of employees. People who have worked hard, who have done what is expected of them, who have been loyal to the organization, and who suddenly find themselves out of a job, or people who are manipulated and exploited in a merger or required to shift to psychological directions which are uncongenial to their equilibrium-maintaining efforts, will feel they have been done an injustice, no matter how much economics may seem to support that action. When enough people experience injustice they will react collectively in response to that feeling.

The major adaptive task for many managers involves coping with the increasing intensity of demand made on them for performance, particularly in organizations whose heads are preoccupied with running them for quarterly reports to security analysts. Top managements, like competitive children, feel they must look good to those whose approval they think they require, and that approval requires straight As on every report card. The need to look good by the numbers now pervades most organizations. Such a focus by top management inevitably means that people are moved up and down an organizational hierarchy like yo-yos, with increasing pressure to make the results look good.

Summary

Adaptation involves coping with one's own character defenses in the face of tasks which are age-specific, stage-specific, and congenial to one's equilibrium-maintaining efforts. Adaptation involves managing the drives, managing the distance between the ego ideal and the self-image, and managing one's focal conflicts in the face of institutional requirements which may magnify or intensify them or, conversely, make them incongruous in a given situation. The leaders of organizations, still relatively unsophisticated psychologically, now must take such issues into account, which intensifies the stress on them. These are dimensions of occupational stress which require our careful attention.

As is already evident from this brief overview of the theory, there are some critical issues to be considered in all managerial relationships and decisions: the meaning and exercise of authority or the role of being a boss; rivalry with peers, superiors, and subordinates; preferred ways of handling aggression, affection, dependency, and one's ego ideal and their relationship to selecting an appropriate position; deciding on promotion or job change; choosing people for jobs; moving people from one place to another; threats to self-esteem in the process of supervision; the degree to which the job meets the requirements of the ego ideal of the person doing it or the collective aspirations of the group; guilt for managerial decisions or the prospect of feeling guilty for hostility to another which interferes with rational decision-making, particularly in performance appraisal; difficulties people have living up to their own severe superegos and their inordinate expectations of themselves; inability of people to change from one style of supervisory behavior to another; difficulties some people have in assuming responsibility; coping with personal obsolescence.

In addition, these considerations will help us to understand the origin of group norms as modes of defense, the importance of the group and organizational goals, and the varying styles of organization and processes of work congenial to different people, and the mobilization of hostility or affection toward management.

Chapter 3

Applications to Management

We turn from explaining the theory to its application in managerial practice around issues of leadership, organizational structure, job design, change, management development, compensation, selection and placement, and supervisory problems.

Leadership

Our theory, building as it does on the earliest feelings about dependency and rivalry, gives leadership a central place. Many contemporary theories, particularly those related to group processes and group dynamics, omit or depreciate the role of the leader or unwittingly undermine the power of the leader in the interests of democratic egalitarianism. But we can now understand that leadership power and managerial style are crucial elements in organizational cohesion and functioning and therefore must be neither denied nor vitiated.

Selection. The person who becomes a natural leader is one who feels himself to be neither the victim of a hostile world nor helplessly inadequate in the face of it. He or she has a solid identification with an authoritative parent of the same sex and other competent models, including the parent of the opposite sex. He feels himself and his models to be approved by the parent of the opposite sex. This personal comfort with self, the basis of flexibility, together with the competences it allows such a person to achieve, enables him to exercise the authority of the parent of the same sex and to generate competence and skill in his followers, whose rivalry he need not fear. He takes pleasure in what he does. A power position is not an end in itself. The ideal candidates for executive roles are persons whose histories have these ideal features.

However, not all of us are so fortunate as to be ideal. In fact, some who experience themselves as helplessly inadequate or fighting a difficult and hostile world seek executive roles as devices in that psychological battle.

One of Winston Churchill's biographers reports that as a schoolboy, unloved by his parents, he was scuffling with his schoolmates. He is reported to have screamed at his tormentors, "One day I shall be a great man and you will be nobodies, then I will stamp and crush you."[14] He is described as having an all-consuming appetite for greatness. Of course, he achieved it.

The person who becomes an executive out of the need to compensate for an unconscious feeling of helplessness seeks power to wield over others. He seeks position as an end in itself because it makes him feel more worthy. Instead of enjoying what he *does*, he anticipates the pleasure he will have in *being* boss. He has much more difficulty in the leadership role because unconsciously he does not feel himself to be powerful and, therefore, capable of dealing with whatever issues may arise. On the contrary, feeling so helpless, he has had to acquire power in order to be able to compensate for his helplessness and to deal with competitors and the hostile environment.

He displaces his anger with himself, the product of a low self-image and a high ego ideal, onto his subordinates, on whom he projects his inadequacies. That mechanism enables him to over-control them, berate them, manipulate them, "whip them into shape," and otherwise attack them. This is the mechanism of displacement. His unconscious position is easy to rationalize: If he is the boss and he feels so inadequate, then by definition those who report to him must be many times more inadequate. He is therefore more likely to be more rivalrous, more rigid, and more controlling, and, therefore, to have greater difficulty developing competence in those who report to him. Churchill is described as having had overweening pride, a tyrannical nature, a lack of concern for subordinates, and an insensate drive for power. He once excused his rudeness to the male nurse who was taking care of him by explaining, "I am a great man."

The managerial world abounds in men and women like this, although most are less extreme. Often they can be highly effective in attaining short-term results as a product of their driving, power-oriented mastery efforts. Such persons find the typical hierarchical bureaucratic model an excellent administrative device, for its rigidities fit their rigidities, its highly rationalized control systems fit their needs to control. Indeed, they often speak of business as a war and themselves akin to generals leading an army. It is not surprising that Churchill had been a military man.

Leaders who have this basic psychological posture find it very difficult to be flexible in changing environments, to share their power with subordinates, and to make use of behavioral science knowledge. By the mechanism of projection, they attribute their own motives to their subordinates. They experience their subordinates as just as rivalrous as they and always waiting to seize their power. Like generals, they seem to have to be hypermasculine in their roles. As they experience it, not to be hypermasculine is to be its polar opposite: feminine. In their distorted perception, to be feminine is to be noncompetitive and once more helpless and blameworthy.

Such a psychological position implies that persons who hold it deny underlying wishes for dependency and, by reaction formation, go to the opposite extreme. They therefore find it difficult to be dependent, however appropriately, on their subordinates or to allow their subordinates to be dependent on them. That difficulty further inhibits their capacity to develop others.

Since disproportionate numbers of such persons seek managerial roles, careful screening for such behavioral qualities and traits must be undertaken. Frequently bright young men and women who have highly competitive characteristics are chosen for their executive promise without weighing how effective they will be when they are required to lead others and build organizations, as contrasted with demonstrating personal competence.

Leadership Style. Organizations in any culture are essentially recapitulations of the family structure in that culture. The characteristic style of leadership in organizations therefore parallels the style of leadership in the family. Thus, any discussion of leadership style is necessarily culture bound.

The United States has been called a child-oriented culture. Increasing numbers of children are encouraged to follow their own interests. The heavy emphasis of parental practice in the United States is on maintaining family cohesion and integrity by means of parental affection, guidance, and support in an interactive mode with children. The basic elements of the ego ideal which American parents hold out usually emphasize: (1) independence—learn to stand on your own feet; (2) flexibility—roll with the punches and come out on top; (3) happiness—enjoy life; and (4) the development of moral and spiritual values—society should be better for your contribution. This is not to say that all parents operate with all children according to these criteria, but they do dominate the American ethos.

There are a number of implications for the leadership role. Obviously, the people reared in a culture in which parents actively foster these values will come to organizations with expectations that those in leadership roles over them will do the same. They are likely to expect that leaders will offer themselves as identification models, will provide support for their subordinates' continued growth toward their ego ideals, and will open avenues for action so that subordinates may master their environments while simultaneously meeting their self-demands for both effectiveness and enhanced self-images. In effect, they bring to the organization unconscious psychological contracts, continuations from family experiences, with certain clauses that they expect to have fulfilled in return for their contributions to the organization.[15] This thrust has become more imperative in recent years as increasing numbers of people have left independent craft, trade, and even professional work to turn to organizations for their livelihood, and as the work organization has taken over many of the functions of the extended family.[16] They thus expect leaders to be concerned with perpetuating the organization, rather than short-term expediency. Concomitantly, as their economic level rises, they are less likely to be predominantly motivated by money.

As a consequence, there is a major and growing tension between what people expect of leadership and the controlling, dominating thrust of the many people who seek power in managerial roles, between the rigidity of hierarchical structure and the need for people to act on problems for their own and the organization's mastery of self and environment, and between short-term profit motives as against perpetuation.

Purpose. Whatever the idiosyncratic style of the leader, he is the central device for holding the organization together and directing it towards its task. He must therefore first define organizational purpose by putting forth his own ego ideal as it relates to the organization. What does he want to achieve during his tenure? What does he want to look back on? What would he want written on his epitaph? Inevitably he is acting on such impulses. If he would make them clear and encourage others in the organization to do the same, the resulting integrated combination would be a statement of organizational purpose which would unite organization members in common bond toward shared ideals.

The president of a major metropolitan department store did exactly this with the ten people who constituted his top management team. He and they adjourned to a rural retreat. With the help of the consultant they spelled out what each wanted to achieve and look back on. After these individual statements were offered, written on large sheets of paper which were hung on the wall, and subsequently discussed, they were consolidated into a comprehensive integrated statement of organizational purpose. One of the crucial issues left out by the group until the president himself brought it in with great emphasis was the fact that theirs was a high quality store and he intended to keep it that way. Each of them was concerned with his own area; only the president could view the whole. He thereby represented not only his ego ideal but what then became the collective ego ideal of the group. The generalized statement then became the guide for organizational planning and a point of reference for making organizational decisions.

Once purpose is defined, it becomes the charter for the organization. Goals then become derivatives of purpose. As a result, goals take on powerful psychological meaning for those who are identified with the purpose. Those who áre not so identified would do well to seek another organization.

In the example just offered it became clear that, given this statement of purpose, the department store would not engage in certain kinds of advertising or sales practices, or handle lower-priced items. Some of the management felt that higher volume and increased profits would follow if the company did not strive so hard for a quality image. Others pointed out that such gains would be short-lived because the department store could not render the services it did and still compete with discount stores in lower price ranges. Those who had to vanquish customers rather than serve them ultimately sought employment elsewhere.

To satisfy the demands of the ego ideal, goals must be high but attainable in steps, so that there is always a sense of moving toward both individual and organizational ego ideals. Within the organization's statement of purpose, there may be many substatements for organization components. Certainly every leader at every level should establish such a contract with those who report to him.

Problem Solving. After purpose has been defined and realistic goals established, the fundamental task of the leader is to use his power wisely and flexibly toward solving organizational problems by mobilizing the energies and resources of his people. He does this in the same manner as the good parent increases the strength of the family and his children as individuals—by confronting his subordinates with the realities the organization faces, what it is up against in the competitive world, and supporting them in the process of learning how to cope with it effectively. In the model of the good father or good teacher, the executive, manager, or supervisor helps his people get an accurate view of the organization's realities and those of their own department or unit, involves them in collective decision-making to the extent to which they are capable of contributing by reason of skill, competence, and knowledge, and fosters their competence in adapting to and coping with reality. He is the core around which the work group coheres.

During a recessionary period, a company president whom I shall call Frank Edsall was faced with the alternatives of putting his entire work force on a four-day week or of putting the manufacturing employees on a four-day week while the salesmen continued to work as before. He was afraid that if he took his salesmen off the road, he would lose sales he badly needed. On the other hand, if he did not require the salesmen to sacrifice in the same way that the other employees did, the others would be angry. No matter which way he turned, there would be a price he did not want to pay. Mr. Edsall called a meeting of all his manufacturing employees and told them what the problems were and some of the alternatives he saw and the dilemma of the choice. He asked them what they wanted to do. The manufacturing employees said they would take the four-day week but they wanted the salesmen to stay on the road because further loss of sales meant the likelihood of further cutbacks in their workweek. Mr. Edsall had faced the problem realistically, had helped them look at the realities both he and they faced, and had made the rational choice. Had he made that choice himself, the likelihood is that they would not have been satisfied because they would not have known all the realities. The likelihood also is that without that knowledge and without deciding about their own fate, they would have acted in a more primitively self-centered way.

The leader must accept aggression and rivalry and redirect that kind of hostility into problem-solving activity. He is simultaneously a model, a teacher, a parental figure, a guide, and an arbiter. He stands for responsibility, integrity, and the creative use of power. Rather than adopting a given management style, he is flexible in his behavior, choosing that kind of behavior which is appropriate to his people, his organization, and the situation in which they find themselves. Just as a parent may have to behave differently with the same child under different circumstances, so the leader may have to behave differently with subordinates. He does not abdicate his power role or apologize for it, but at the same time he does not wield it as a weapon for his own gratification. Nor does he feel guilty for having and using power. That feeling usually underlies abdication, or the complete abandonment of power to the subordinate, which in turn results in various kinds of panic behavior often more characteristic of gangs or fraternities, which is self-centered, hedonistic, and defensive.

Basic Processes. There are three basic processes which go on in individuals to which leadership must attend. These are strivings to fulfill needs for *ministration, maturation,* and *mastery.* [17]

Ministration refers to gratification of dependency needs or the need to have them gratified. All of us have dependency needs of varying degrees. They are at their maximum in infancy and in old age, but they are nevertheless present throughout life. In an organizational situation these are met by an adequate definition of the task, adequate guidance and direction, adequate orientation, functional policies and practices, protective fringe benefits, and supportive social relationships. Maturation refers to the need for increasing one's capacities and skills and for continued development toward being a mature, capable adult. Mastery refers to the need to act as an adult, to be able to come close to one's ego ideal, to have an effect on one's fate and the determination of one's life direction.

Competences. Meeting these needs, to the extent they can be met in an organization, is the fundamental task of the leader. That takes three kinds of competence. In multiple studies of effective leadership it has been demonstrated that effective leaders show *managerial competence,* that is, effectiveness in competing in the external world, in coping with it, and in leading their organizations to adaptive achievement. [18] They also show *technical competence,* having understanding of the technical processes unique to the organization or unit and being able to further the development of that competence on behalf of the organization. Furthermore, they have *human relations competence.* One may view leadership in a different way: proactive behavior, which means acting on the external world and pulling the organization into adaptive efforts with respect to it; mediative behavior, or maintaining the internal equilibrium of the organization while it is adapting to its external environment; and homeostatic behavior, the capacity for relieving and releasing tensions within the organization to free energy for cooperative adaptive efforts rather than destructive internal competition.[19]

The extremely proactive or managerial leader who is less attuned to homeostatic and mediative roles or to technical and human relations competences becomes a charismatic leader who maximizes his own self-interest but leaves behind an organization incapable of adapting without him. This is the characteristic posture of the entrepreneur, or a de Gaulle. The executive who is technically powerful but who cannot give adequate managerial leadership or human relations leadership ultimately is unable to manage or compete, and despite the technical competence of his organization, he does not make it an adaptive one. The mediative leader who gives disproportionate emphasis to human relations considerations fails to cope with either managerial or technical problems. Frequently his is a paternalistic emphasis on being nice, which fails to provide adequate attention to people's needs to grow and become more competent. His need to please others keeps him from maintaining high standards and from getting the work of the organization done effectively. He puts subordinates in a double bind: He frustrates them, but how can they become angry with such a nice guy?

In most organizations human relations problems are dealt with as an afterthought, an added burden to the organization which is incidental to its central thrust. They are, therefore, most frequently dealt with by a buying-off process, as in fringe benefits, by a game-playing process, as in many kinds of organizational development activities, or by simple abandonment, as in leaving employee requirements solely to the bargaining table.

The concept of leadership I have just enunciated is frequently seen by more aggressive men, particularly those who are compensating for their underlying feelings of helplessness by fighting a perceived hostile world, as passive and feminine. On the contrary, it is a highly active, demanding one, requiring as it does interaction and leadership rather than command. This concept becomes increasingly imperative as it becomes more difficult in contemporary organizations to command rather than to lead. With higher levels of education, fewer people allow themselves to be commanded. With an increasingly differentiated marketplace, decision-making must be pushed to lower levels in the organization. Such a concept is especially imperative in established organizations which must constantly fight the tendencies to become ossified, to maximize dependency, and to lean heavily on yesterday's solutions to yesterday's problems. In short, the leader makes clear his purposes, goals, and objectives. He clarifies how he would reach them. He insists that subordinates contribute to the formulation of purpose, goals, and means. He maintains high standards so that goals may be viewed as worthy. He maintains three kinds of leadership competence. By doing so he demonstrates that he cares about his subordinates and builds trust. When he does so the leader becomes an identification model for those who directly or indirectly report to him.

In chapter one, I discussed the identification process. There are several implications of that process. As long as people have a need to continuously increase their adaptive competence, they will continue emulating those who have greater power or competence, one way or another, than they have. Thus, we are always pursuing models and seeking to become better, no matter how good we have become. It is this phenomenon which makes identification with the leader at whatever level a crucial one. That is, followers or subordinates must be able to identify with their leaders in order to learn from them, to evolve those values appropriate to the organization in which they work and to the discipline they follow, and to acquire through the medium of that identification further identification with the organization which the leader represents.

To emasculate leadership by misguided organizational development efforts which seek to vitiate power differentials undermines the acquisition of authoritative competence on the part of the followers. There is no point in being like the foreman or vice president if he is but a helpless patsy.

Design of Organizational Structure

Most discussions of leadership fail to relate leadership style, and thereby a theory of personality, to organizational structure. Sociological discussions of organizational structure rarely touch on the relationship of structure to leadership. In my view they are closely intertwined. Indeed, organizational structure is assumed to be a given and in turn implicitly assumes autocratic leadership and passive followers of undifferentiated personalities.

Historic Model. Most organizational structures are simply the historic bureaucratic model of the church and the army, operating on a chain-of-command basis in which roles are defined, authority and responsibility allocated, and formal distances maintained between levels. Historically organizations have been built around this model as if it were the equivalent of the human spine, that is, a fixed universal entity. It is not. To operate on that basis, to assume that every organization should have a manufacturing unit, a sales unit, an accounting unit, and so forth, is to evolve and perpetuate a rigidity. Usually also the more formal the structure, the greater the network of informal ways of accomplishing what has to be done, as in the military. The presence of a powerful informal organization in the context of a formal structure is an indication of how poorly the formal structure itself adapts to reality.

While there must be distribution of authority and responsibility as well as accountability, one need not start with a given structure for accomplishing these ends. If adaptation or mastery of the environment is the crucial issue for the perpetuation of the organization, as it is for the individual, then one must begin by defining the aspect of the environment to be mastered and developing a strategy for doing so. As Paul R. Lawrence and Jay W. Lorsch have pointed out, the organizational structure can then be built to accomplish that task.[20] The greater the rapidity of change in the environment, the more flexible the organizational structure will have to be. Similarly, the more stable the environment to which the organization addresses itself and the narrower its function with respect to that environment, the more likely that the organization will be rather formally structured.

Dominant Competitive Edge. Organizational structure should begin with the definition of the organization's dominant competitive edge: What can it or might it do better than others? What is its self-defined niche? What task must be accomplished to sustain that edge? Having defined the organization's task, one can work backward from that task to evolve functional units to accomplish components of that task. Within those units functional roles can be structured which often may transcend characteristic functions, such as sales or engineering. For example, in many contemporary organizations, the sales task is carried out by teams of technical people who engage with teams of similar people in the customer's organization.

Power. Having defined the organizational task and the roles necessary to accomplish that task, it is imperative to allocate adequate power to the managerial and supervisory roles so that those who occupy them can serve as adequate models for their subordinates. This means not only a range of authority commensurate with responsibility, but also, as Elliott Jaques and Wilfred Brown have pointed out, authority to veto the appointment of their subordinates by others.[21]

Integration. The organizational structure should provide modes of integrating diverse functions, whether by integrative persons, by superiors, or by internal mechanisms for resolving conflict. It should also be possible for different kinds of units to be organized differently according to their differing needs and functions.

Negotiation and Appeal. In addition, there should be continuing processes of redefining role boundaries among persons and units as it becomes necessary to reallocate responsibilities and redefine activities in keeping with changes in the marketplace and environment.

Jaques and Brown have recommended that there be a continuous appeals process through which any employee may appeal the decision of a superior up through the head of the organization. The combination of continuous role negotiation, an appeals process, and a legislative process through which people agree on rules, policies, and procedures for accomplishing the task, contributes to minimizing both the depressive and the paranoid positions mentioned in chapter one by increasing people's capacity to act on their own problems, by narrowing some of the distance between employees and management, by decreasing the unknowns about higher management levels, by allowing people to have significant influence on their own fate and that of the organization without, at the same time, undermining the authority structure or leading to leadership abdication.

The opportunity to modify organizational structure and role continuously in keeping with current competitive conditions requires that people continuously face reality, which counteracts fantasy and the tendency to deny reality by ignoring it or wishing it would go away. Facing reality militates against helpless dependency and the accompanying resentment and anger. It counteracts obsolescence. It minimizes political machinations. Unfortunately, in traditional bureaucratic organizations, many people are compelled to become experts in playing the system and in acquiring power within the system for their own aggrandizement.

Psychological Qualities. Once a structure has been defined, the major organizational task may be redefined into occupational roles, which in turn may then be examined for their psychological qualities. Lawrence and Lorsch have suggested several dimensions for doing this—one of which is personality or the temperament required to do the job.[22] Lorsch and John J. Morse point out that only when a three-way match is present among members' characteristics, the unit's internal environment, and its external environment can there be effective unit performance with individuals feeling competent.[23] The task of refining the psychological aspects of role requirements becomes more complex as work roles themselves become more complex.

From the orientation I have presented here, one may view any task around four dimensions: (1) What avenues does it require or permit for the expression of aggression? Does the person have to attack problems vigorously himself? Does he or she have to persuade or command others? Does he have to constrain his own impulses and mediate others' differences? Does he have to be passively pleasing? (2) What avenues does it require or permit for affection, the need to love and be loved? Does the person work closely with others and therefore have to be sociable? Or does he work alone, without such relationships? Is he required to be emotionally distant from superiors or subordinates? Does he have to be the target of other people's aggression and therefore be unliked? The four modes of managing the drives as schematized in Figure 7 might be helpful in thinking about these questions. (3) How much dependency does he have to handle? Does he have many subordinates dependent on him? Is he responsible for the lives of one or many people, as a surgeon or an airplane pilot? Is there a network of interdependent relationships so that he can count on support? (4) What ego ideal demands does it fulfill? That is, for what kind of a person at what stage in his career, at what age, and with what value system does this task constitute a step toward fulfilling deeply held aspirations? Put another way, what kind of a person would like himself for accomplishing what this particular task requires to be accomplished? What are the intrinsic satisfactions to be derived from the task and what psychological significance does the financial compensation have?

Managing Organizational Change

From a psychoanalytic point of view, the course of development is, among other things, one of building up a range of memory images. We make a part of ourselves those persons, places, and things that have significance for us. We develop ties to those objects both by repetitive contacts and by means of the memory images of them which we hold. These ties and images constitute our social networks and provide the psychological support for our growth and development as well as for our mastery of ourselves and our environment. When they are broken, the self-image is lowered because the feeling of helplessness is increased. Everyone who has moved from one place to another or from one job to another, no matter how desirable or advantageous such a move might have been, knows the disruptive experience of that change. All change is a loss experience.

Loss. While many people cope with loss experiences by simply denying them, pretending that they are not painful or ignoring the pain, for most people they create a feeling of depression. One loses preferred modes of attaining and giving affection, handling aggression, dependency needs—those familiar routines which we have evolved and take for granted. In addition, loss precipitates physical illness; recent studies indicate that life-threatening illnesses and sudden coronary death are precipitated by loss experiences. Thomas H. Holmes and his colleagues at the University of Washington have worked out a weighted scale (see Figure 9) to reflect the impact of various life changes as precipitants of illnesses and accidents.[24]

Loss is a difficult experience to handle. Some have greater difficulty than others adapting to loss, particularly if what one has left behind is psychologically important. All loss must be mourned and the attendant feelings disgorged if a restitution process is to operate effectively. Most organizational change flounders because the experience of loss is not taken into account. When the threats of loss are so severe as to increase peoples' sense of helplessness, their ability to master themselves and their environments decreases. To undertake successful organizational change, an executive must anticipate and provide means of working through that loss.

Adaptation. Ralph G. Hirschowitz, building on the work of J. S. Tyhurst, delineates the experience of loss as a four-stage process.[25]

(1) *Impact* is the stage in which the news of change is received. The reaction is one of daze and shock, most intense if the change is undesired and unexpected. In such cases, the reaction starts with emergency fight-fright-flight response (fight: "They can't do that to me;" fright: "Help! They're doing it to me;" flight: "I've got to get out of here"). Caught between these three, the person may "freeze." Or he may become disoriented, erratic,

Rank	Life Event	Scale of Impact
1	Death of spouse	100
2	Divorce	73
3	Marital separation	65
4	Jail term	63
5	Death of close family member	63
6	Personal injury or illness	53
7	Marriage	50
8	Fired at work	47
9	Marital reconciliation	45
10	Retirement	45
11	Change in health of family member	44
12	Pregnancy	40
13	Sex difficulties	39
14	Gain of new family member	39
15	Business readjustment	39
16	Change in financial state	38
17	Death of close friend	37
18	Change to different line of work	36
19	Change in number of arguments with spouse	35
20	Mortgage over $10,000	31
21	Foreclosure of mortgage or loan	30
22	Change in responsibilities at work	29
23	Son or daughter leaving home	29
24	Trouble with in-laws	29
25	Outstanding personal achievement	28
26	Wife begins or stops work	26
27	Begin or end school	26
28	Change in living conditions	25
29	Revision of personal habits	24
30	Trouble with boss	23
31	Change in work hours or conditions	20
32	Change in residence	20
33	Change in schools	20
34	Change in recreation	19
35	Change in church activities	19
36	Change in social activities	18
37	Mortgage or loan less than $10,000	17
38	Change in sleeping habits	16
39	Change in number of family get-togethers	15
40	Change in eating habits	15
41	Vacation	13
42	Christmas	12
43	Minor violations of the law	11

Source: T. H. Holmes and R. H. Rahe, "The Social Readjustment Rating Scale," *Journal of Psychosomatic Research* 11:213-218 (1967).

Figure 9. Social Readjustment Rating Scale

and distractable. Impaired perception is common, and in severe crisis, he may mimic an acutely confused state. This phase lasts from a few hours to a few days.

(2) *Recoil-Turmoil* follows impact and is the phase in which the person searches for what he has lost. He is at this point exploring the implications of his loss, detaching from what is familiar, and beginning to scan the horizon for some kind of replacement. His reactions, which include rage, anxiety, depression, guilt, and shame, may be expressed openly, as in weeping, or concealed behind facades of overcontrol and detachment. During this period he regains some of his normal mental patterns, but the effect on his vitality is still depressive. This phase lasts from several days to several weeks, depending on the nature and extent of the change and the degree of the person's own attachment to what he has lost.

(3) *Adjustment* is the period in which the person begins to recover from the negative aspects of his change. Having completed most of his detachment tasks, he now begins to explore new relationships, examine problems facing him in his new environment, and test solutions to those problems. His painful feelings diminish and gradually give way to some hope about the future. We now hear phrases like, "All is not lost," and "Life must go on." His time is occupied in learning new ways, acquiring new knowledge, skills, and routines. This phase can last two to four weeks, but longer if the environment is particularly uncertain or if the person is confused with only vague ideas of what is to be.

(4) *Reconstruction* begins when the person has completely relinquished his past and moved well into the problem-solving required of him in his new position. He has replaced what he lost and is now in the process of attaching himself to the new elements and testing their nature and boundaries. This period may last for a matter of months.

People cannot reach optimal productivity, says Dr. Hirschowitz, until they have completed this transition sequence in its entirety. From an emotional standpoint, the most critical period lasts from the first day to the first week or so of the adjustment period.

This pattern can be seen in the behavior of people who lose their jobs. Douglas H. Powell and Paul F. Driscoll describe the four-stage process that people who lose their jobs go through.[26] Their first experience is relaxation and relief. Interest in job-hunting is minimal. Second, a period of concerted effort begins in about twenty-five days, after boredom and edginess have arisen. At this point a person starts a systematic search for work. Support and encouragement from family and friends and job openings are a person's major needs. Third, a period of vacillation and doubt will set in if the usual ways of getting a job have not worked. The person may become intensely moody and anxious. Relationships with family and friends deteriorate. The person begins to question his professional identity. Without counseling, a person at this stage may defeat himself by conveying his self-doubts to prospective employers. Fourth, a period of malaise and cynicism may set in for about six weeks. A person loses his sense of control over his own life. Now he looks for a job only occasionally and avoids personal contact with prospective employers. He needs professional help to restore his self-confidence.

These phenomena highlight the underlying psychological processes which occur in all change. They are the fundamental forces with which anyone who tries to bring about organizational change must deal if he wishes to sustain the momentum of the organization and reduce resistance to the change process.

The Change Process Exemplified

Organizational change is best effected when people have a clear understanding of why the change is necessary, opportunity to critically cross-examine the leader and verify for themselves the necessity for change, occasions to mourn the loss of the old which must be given up, and modes of action by which they themselves can participate in the change.

Step 1. For example, in one major company the president met with some eighty of his subordinates for three days. On the first day, he described to them the history and development of the organization, where it stood now, and where it had to go in order to compete effectively.

Step 2. Following his presentation the large group was divided into small, cross-functional groups, so that participants could discuss the president's speech and clarify questions to bring back to the plenary session for response by the president. This particular process made it possible for everybody in the management group to face the contemporary realities. In the process of critically examining what the president had to say, they had a chance to mourn and regret, but at the same time began to mobilize themselves in the restitution process.

Step 3. The next step was a report by outside experts on future socioeconomic trends, which was followed by more small group discussion and questions. Such a report confirmed from outside sources the realities that the president was calling to their attention and further counteracted the denial mechanism.

Step 4. Next they were asked to discuss in small groups the implications of what they had heard from the outsiders for their own organizations. Following those discussions the conclusions of the small groups were summarized for the information of the total group. This set the restitution process in further motion in the direction of action.

Step 5. They were then asked, on the basis of the implications they had formulated, who should do what about them. Another set of small group conclusions was then summarized for the larger group.

Step 6. Following these sessions, the management group was divided into functional groupings to outline specific implications for the respective organizational functions. These conclusions were summarized and put into a book for the guidance of all of the participants and their managerial action. They agreed to carry the discussion to their own subordinates and to get feedback from those people on further questions, problems, and implications.

Step 7. After a year of working on the organizational changes, the president held another meeting. This time he reviewed what he had said earlier and where things stood presently. Once again this review was subject to question and examination in small groups. Questions now were addressed to the whole top management group.

Step 8. Next, there were two days of conceptual teaching

about contemporary leadership methods and styles, followed by small group discussion about these presentations.

Step 9. This was then followed by a discussion of the question, "How does the organizational structure and its processes have to be changed in order to facilitate your acting in your leadership roles in the ways we are expecting of you?" Small group discussions evolved a good many suggestions for change processes which were then summarized. Some could be immediately undertaken by top management, others by functional heads, and still others required considerably more study and careful examination.

Step 10. Once again this was followed by meetings of functional groups which discussed the implications for their activities.

Step 11. Annual review meetings will make the change process a continuous one conducted by those who will be most affected by it and who have firsthand familiarity with the problems of bringing the changes about.

Effective organizational change usually means thinking through the underlying psychological assumptions behind the changes. Since there is some assumption about motivation behind every organizational action, policy, procedure, and structure, that assumption has to be made clear or there could be unexpected and undesirable consequences.

Because of the need to clarify assumptions, which are usually least evident to those who hold them, and because organizational change inevitably involves a great degree of turmoil, effective change usually requires the use of an external consultant well versed in the psychological matters discussed here. Such a person is in an objective position, outside the turmoil and the power structure, and can be a helpful guide when emotional turmoil is likely to cloud decision-making and temporarily disrupt relationships. The professional contacts provide reassurance which is particularly necessary when the organizational structure is in a fluid state. Further, in a period of turmoil and change, closer and more frequent contacts are required between managers and the people who report to them.

This is not to say that executives cannot change structural or procedural arrangements in an organization by themselves. Obviously they can and do. But most such changes undermine morale, slow momentum, and alienate people. Usually they have only short-term positive effects. Effective, adaptive organizational change is a long-term process which includes the necessity to deal with the many psychological issues.

Organization Development. In recent years human relations have been tackled under the rubric of organization development, which includes confrontation groups, T-groups, communications activities, survey-feedback, and other modes of facilitating interpersonal and intergroup relations. Each of these has its place, but all are limited to the extent that they assume that people can make use of rational information and that motivation is primarily conscious. If both of these conditions were sufficient, most people would already have solved their problems. Thus, organization development consultants who assume people need only information to act rationally are likely to leave many problems unsolved. In fact, sometimes they do more harm than good.[27]

Most organization development processes cannot deal with the idiosyncrasies of the leadership and the problems which make it difficult for leadership to implement the kinds of changes that are required. Self-centered leadership, exploitative leadership, and hyperaggressive leadership all arise from motivations which have deep psychological sources. These leaders will have great difficulty effecting change which is adaptive for their organizations. The same is true of dependent leaders or leaders who cannot make decisions or be forthright. These conditions and problems are not dealt with by the techniques that organization development usually offers. One needs psychological understanding to be able to work with the people who must do the implementing.

In addition, one cannot get an objective view of people's feelings from inside the organization. People guard and protect themselves. If they expose themselves, then frequently they may feel guilty and withdraw into further self-protection. The understanding and interpretation of such feelings requires the same kind of psychological sophistication as the understanding and interpretation of any other subtle or complex phenomenon. They simply are not amenable to being understood by people who have two weeks or two months of training. Many group experiences intended to lead to openness and trust merely are devices through which people can express sadistic hostility after having learned to use the buzz words. Many consultants are unaware of this way of exploiting group experiences. Even the managerial participants themselves may remain unaware of it. Such sadistic exploitation creates psychological wounds and strengthens barriers.

Group process experiences have important usefulness in coping with change. People need to understand process, that is, what goes on among people in groups and how it goes on. In addition, they should know what kind of impact they have on others, which is frequently most easily learned in groups. It is important to learn modes and techniques of conducting meetings, of getting feedback, of communicating with people, of interviewing, and so on. However, like all intellectual learning experiences and those of a superficial emotional kind, these techniques are limited. They are useful in the service of comprehensive activity, just as knowledge about good diet, self-examination, taking blood tests, and things of that kind are helpful in maintaining one's own health. However, when it comes to doing something to sustain health, such as surgery, medication, or other forms of treatment, one wants expert understanding and knowledge.

Psychological Contract. Perhaps it becomes easier to understand why such careful attention must be given to organizational change when one realizes, as I mentioned in chapter 1, that people choose organizations to work in which fit their psychological needs. However unconsciously they do this, they form bonds with organizations and develop expectations of how organizations should behave toward them.[28] Organizations foster such expectations not only by the kind of work they do, but also by the attitudes they take toward their employees, the benefits and services they provide, and the ideologies they hold forth. In effect, people and organizations form unconscious psychological contracts. I have called the process of fulfilling such psychological contracts *reciprocation*. When one or another party to that contract unilaterally violates it, then the other reacts with all of the anger and frustration that usually follows an experience of being unfairly treated. The striking feature of the psychological contract is that nowhere is it written. But if each party tacitly assumes that such a contract exists, each expects the other to act in keeping with it.

For example, at the time of a study there, the Kansas Power and Light Company had a tradition of paying its employees good but not spectacular salaries. It did not press them for continuous hard work. Its practices assured them that once on the payroll they were likely to be able to retain their jobs unless they could not do the work. They could not expect to advance fast or to earn as much as aircraft workers in Wichita, but their jobs were more secure. In fact, many people went to work in that company for the presumed security. In return, without specifying their expectations in writing, the company anticipated that when there were bitter snowstorms and the lines were down, their people would be willing to leave warm beds to repair the lines. That is, they expected their people to be identified with the service the company had to render. When an employee injured himself off the job and could no longer work at his old duties, the other employees expected the company to find a place for him. When it did not, they protested to company officers, to local service clubs, and others until the company did. Even though the company had no formal or legal obligation, it reemployed him.

Note that those who sought employment in this company would tend to be people whose dependency needs were such that they were comfortable having a regular job for life as contrasted with competing in an open market with frequent ups and downs. They were more likely to have powerful superegos which were gratified in rendering service to others. Therefore, they were also more likely to expect the company to meet both superego and dependency needs. When, in this instance, it failed to do both, they regarded that as a contractual violation. The company might well feel a psychological contract had been violated if they failed to render conscientious service, for its dependence on them was almost as powerful as theirs on it.

The same issues are present whenever there is organizational change. Unconsciously, and even consciously, people have bargained for one contract which is then unilaterally changed when they are reassigned, terminated, moved, or given new responsibilities or reporting relationships.

The implication of this is that the process of change is ideally a process of continually renegotiating that psychological contract. That is, employees and management together should be continuously revising organizational structure, procedures, processes, and functions in keeping with continuously changing environmental requirements and demands.

They should be asking these questions as they meet together: What are we up against? What problems and conflicts occur repetitively? What can we do about them? What are the people who report to us up against? What kind of help do they need from us? Why are we doing what we are doing (policy, procedure, process)? What outcome do we expect by doing it this way? What assumptions about motivation are we making when we do it this way to get the outcome? How valid are those assumptions? What would we have to do differently, and how, to act more closely in keeping with more valid psychological assumptions?

To illustrate, characteristically, when sales territories become imbalanced due to population changes or other consumer forces, sales managers usually arbitrarily realign them and reset compensation schemes to fit the new alignments. Usually, they succeed only in making the salesmen feel they have been treated arbitrarily, with accompanying resentment. Sometimes it takes years to relieve the resentment, and sometimes people just quit. The sales manager is implicitly assuming that the salesmen are motivated by money alone and that if they are making less in their new territories or by the new compensation schedule, they will respond by working harder to produce more income. He also expects the salesmen still to be loyal to the company despite his arbitrary way of dealing with them. He and they might both do better if he were to tell them the reasons which indicate a need for change and ask them how they want to cope with it. The first behavior is based on reward-punishment assumptions, the second on an understanding of ego ideal/self-image issues, which leads to increased mastery of the environment and a chance to have an effect on what is happening.

A leader cannot always ask people what they want, but he can understand he is always dealing with an implicit psychological contract whose violation results in loss experiences which compound the losses brought about by change.

The American Oil Company closed a small obsolete refinery in Neodesha, Kansas. A year before they did so, they sent an executive to the community and plant who announced the projected closing. Each employee was interviewed for possible transfer to another refinery or to ascertain his skills for other local jobs. Other companies were solicited for possible job openings. The refinery site was turned over to the community for an industrial park. The company helped the community find other industries for the park. When the change was completed, 300 people were employed where 200 had been before, and everyone, working together, had been able to adapt to the change successfully. The company wasn't being altogether charitable. It had closed another refinery in Louisiana earlier without doing something like this and had felt the repercussions through the influence of that state's senator. When a company is concerned about perpetuation, it soon learns that it cannot do with short-term expedient solutions.

Relationships are fundamental to human existence. Both parties must continually work at sustaining and adapting the relationship to their needs. If they do not, ultimately their relationship fails. The same principles hold true in the relationship between a person and the organization in which he works. When a valued relationship fails, the resulting anger and depression affect not only the mental health of the individuals but also the effectiveness of the organization. In their anger and depression they may well be so preoccupied that they are unable to adapt to the new situation. They may strike or merely passively resist whatever changes are introduced. The contractual problem becomes more severe as people become more dependent on the organization through long service and specialized skills. That was one of the major points of my earlier discussion of aging and obsolescence. With age people become more fearful of threats to that relationship and more subtly hostile in their resistance to and reaction against it.

Implications for Management Development

The chief agent of management development in any organization is the person to whom any employee reports. But there are others. Just as a developing child has opportunities to identify with significant older children and adults as well as with his parents, people who move up within an organization usually have been taken under the wing of a senior person who helps socialize them into the organization, arranges experiences to increase their skills and competences, and guides them through political mazes.

The Mentor. When executives talk about their career progress, usually they will speak about someone in the organization who was "like a father to me." That person, frequently described as a mentor, both shows the junior person much of what he must learn to do as a manager and plugs him into the informal organizational network. One of the major barriers to advancement by women and minority group members is the fact that they so rarely have mentors. This makes it difficult for them to learn many managerial skills and to become part of the informal communications network. No matter what is taught in business schools, much of management is still an art and must be learned through the medium of apprentice-master relationships.

However, sometime around the age of 38 to 40 or so, according to the research of Daniel Levinson, who calls this the "BOOM" experience, people rebel against their mentors.[29] This is part of the middle-age crisis and represents a final effort on the part of the subordinate to free himself of dependency on older, more powerful figures and to assert himself. Like the adolescent, he breaks off his relationship with his mentor, using any excuse which he can rationalize. Some succeed in their self-assertion and go on to greater independence; others flounder at this time and plateau into a defeated position, often with chronic low-level depression.

The mentor may vary as a manager moves from one part of the company to another. However, such a person must be concerned about meeting the ministration, maturation, and mastery needs of his subordinates. He may do some of this personally; he may do much of it in connection with a management development department or a similar activity. But unless the participants in a management development activity know that what is being taught is consistent with what is approved by their superiors, the teaching will be largely a waste of time.

Developmental Programs for the Intimacy Phase. Management development activities should be varied according to the career stage and the life stage of the individual, both of which will be discussed in greater detail later. For example, in the period roughly from 21 to 35, which Erikson refers to as the phase of intimacy (see chapter one), a young person is developing his own track record, acquiring the skills necessary to do a managerial job and the conceptual knowledge to support his skills. This is the same stage of life during which he has the greatest energy, spontaneity, and creativity. Management development activities, therefore, should be directed not only to the acquisition of competence and skills as a foundation for a managerial career, but also should involve his participation in looking critically at the activities of the enterprise. Young people may evolve new ideas of adaptation, and they should undertake experiences which make it possible to test some of those ideas and practices. Too many management development activities offered to people who are in this stage, like the rote teaching of young children, fail to stimulate spontaneous creativity. Thus the opportunity for developing flexible and innovative adaptation is lost.

Preconscious thoughts and fantasies are always rising to the surface, like bubbles in a carbonated beverage. These are the sources of our creativity. When we bubble in the context of problems to be solved, creative solutions arise. However, to continue the analogy, when we are bottled up—as with too many rigid controls or tasks which limit our contribution to solving problems—then we cannot take advantage of our bubbling. In terms of management development, this means that when people are being rotated through jobs to become acquainted with the many facets and functions of an organization, they should continue to be closely in touch with superiors who can take advantage of their fresh, outside views of that function. They also should have the opportunity to do some major task alone, in order that both they and the organization might know how they handle their dependency needs and with what range of independence they can operate comfortably. This information will be particularly important both to them and to the organization in making career choices and deciding on assignments.

In the early part of this period, roughly 21 to 25, many young people are undergoing a moratorium.[30] That is, they are trying to crystallize their identity, to decide who they are and what they should be doing. Career counseling is most important at this point. It is especially valuable if it is built on work experiences which provide the person with a way of measuring himself against the work he has done and assessing his own capacities and limits. Rotational assignments and the opportunity to talk freely with a mentor are particularly important.

Rotation for development usually fails this purpose because it is done without adequate consideration for the person or the learning experience per se. A rotation site should be selected only because there is something specific a person can learn there. He should be at that site only as long as it takes him to learn that. To keep a person six weeks in a transitional job that he learns in two days, or two years in one he learns in a few weeks, is demoralizing.

Rotation for single women in this age range is a particularly sensitive problem. This is the prime time for finding a husband. To be assigned to a suburban or rural area is frequently experienced as being banished from necessary contacts with men.

Few management development programs take into account the need for the prospective manager to understand the psychology of leadership and supervision, as outlined earlier. Most managers are thrown into their roles with no preparation for supervision: how to understand the father-figure aspects of leadership; feelings of guilt and rivalry; problems of managing aggression, affection, dependency, and the ego ideal; the experiences of loss and change; and the psychological contract.

Given the pressures of the gap between the ego ideal and the self-image, people in the intimacy stage, where they are also establishing a track record, need the opportunity to act. To support their self-images, they must establish for themselves and others their capacity to have an effect, to master their environments. If they are not able to demonstrate to themselves that they can do so, they are likely to leave for other jobs. If they stay in the same organization, they will remain restless and impatient until they can prove to themselves that they are capable. I have seen highly successful, highly paid executives take early retirement, particularly from staff positions, to manage businesses of their own just to prove to themselves they could do it.

Management development activities should protect young people from excessive economic and political risk. While feeling impelled to act, younger people recognize the considerable risk of making a mistake. This is the point at which a mentor who will give them permission to take risks and make mistakes becomes particularly important. That mentor in turn must protect them when they fail or they will simply learn not to take risks again. When an organization is overcontrolled to prevent risk-taking and mistakes, when people learn not to err, organizations become stultified and fail to adapt. Thus, coaching is a critical aspect of management development at this period.

Developmental Programs for the Generativity Phase. In the period roughly from 35 to 55, the stage of generativity, or middle age, management development activities should be directed more to helping managers understand their role in the development of others and increasing their capacities for mediating the demands of younger people, on the one hand, and the organization, on the other.

The middle-aged manager frequently must start younger people in career directions. He himself needs support and guidance to do so. In particular he needs the opportunity to deal with problems of rivalry which occur because the ancient oedipal struggle is revived: the younger man always threatens the position of the older man, no matter how good the relationship. The second problem he must deal with is that of guilt. The magical thinking of childhood surfaces whenever one thinks his aggressive actions are likely to hurt someone. As indicated in chapter one, for the small child to think something is the same as to do it. If to be critical is the same as to be hostile and to be hostile is the same as destroying a person, then few people will be able to evaluate performance effectively. This is exactly what happens. Most performance appraisal efforts fail because of the unconscious guilt appraisers feel, which inhibits them, or causes them to distort their appraisals, or both.

A major focus for the development of middle-aged managers in the generativity stage is the understanding of their role as mentor and their own problem with that issue. They usually need particular help to understand the dependency problems of subordinates, the difference between participation and abdication, and the need of younger subordinates to have the opportunity to act. Often, too, middle-aged managers will have learned to survive in an organization which has rewarded conformity; they will have great difficulty learning to let their subordinates be more free than they were permitted to be.

All of these issues are best dealt with in group discussion built around lectures which define some of the issues in general and explore the personal feelings and experiences of the participants.

Particular attention should be given to upgrading the managerial skills of middle-aged people, of providing refresher courses and other means of keeping them in touch with what goes on in the world. These activities are best done in companies or within company groups because it is extremely difficult to get middle-aged people to take isolated academic courses as individuals, even if the company pays for them. They have difficulty tolerating the lowered self-image which goes with being less perfect than they think they ought to be and they need to be, a situation which is likely to occur in the classroom.

Many find participation in brief management development programs on university campuses to be helpful. These serve to renew and refresh skills, to obtain perspectives on other organizations, and to reflect on oneself away from familiar surroundings and undistracted by everyday demands. When such programs extend more than two weeks or so, they in effect become sabbatical periods, which some executives have been advocating.[31]

Before managers leave an organization for outside learning experiences, their superiors should discuss with them why they are being sent, what the company is to gain from their experience, and what they will do upon their return. Managers left in limbo can be quite anxious, which interferes with their learning. When they return, they should have similar conversations with their bosses and perhaps even report to others in the organization new ideas which might be useful for the organization.

Development activity for middle-aged managers should also include the opportunity for people at that level to be able to talk about the problems of being middle-aged, to help them deal with what is known as the middle-age crisis.[32] That crisis arises when adults suddenly discover that half of their lives has already been lived (at about thirty-six for men, since the average life expectancy of the American male is about seventy-two), and the time ahead of them is likely to be shorter than the time now behind them. In addition they are becoming psychologically and physiologically less able to compete in a competitive society. They are being passed by others who are younger than they are. Their skill and knowledge have become more obsolete, and they become more fearful of technical advances and organizational changes. Group discussions and other ways of recognizing the reality of these events, of mourning the losses and of evolving ways to cope with them, is a crucially important part of management development activity at this career point.

When people suddenly become aware of the limited time now available to them, they begin to rethink their lives and what they want to do with their remaining years. An important part of development in the middle years therefore is the opportunity to rethink one's future. For many people this means thinking of a second career. Most people are compelled to make choices among various career alternatives and to emphasize certain values over others early in their career. For example, it is more important for most people aspiring to a managerial career to be more concerned with building their careers than undertaking activities for the public good. In later years, many are more likely to be concerned with their families or conservation. This shift, at a time when one has established himself in a given career and obtained what gratification is available from it, usually requires taking up a second career.

This issue has become more pressing in recent years as many organizations have shrunk, casting aside older managers in favor of younger ones. Left to their own devices, in later years these once-useful men and women have little with which to continue to demonstrate adulthood.

It has been argued that companies should provide credits for time in the organization to apply to retraining for new careers once a person has been passed over for promotion.[33] At the least I believe all organizations should provide mid-career counseling so that executives or managers may readily shift as it becomes timely for them to do so. In addition, such counseling would be excellent preparation for making pre-retirement choices and plans that would ease the burden of that crisis.

Special attention should be given to women managers at this point. Women who have begun to move up in the organization are now very much also involved in supervising and developing others. However, subordinates have different expectations of women than they have of men superiors, stemming from their earliest experiences with their parents. Since people bring into supervisory situations attitudes developed from their earliest relationships with power, it is imperative for both men and women managers to understand this. It is particularly important for women managers to understand that they are likely to fail if they try to act as they think men would act in a given situation. Management development programs should concentrate on enhancing the wish and the need of a woman manager to act like a woman. This does not mean a prescribed set of behaviors, but it does mean that, having evolved a sexual identification in the course of her lifetime, she should be encouraged to be comfortable with that identification and to act naturally in the managerial role.

There is a great deal of evidence about the meaning of mid-life to women in terms of menopause and the departure of grown children to form their own families and develop their own careers. Classically, this has been the "empty nest" phenomenon, which has considerable impact because of its implication that the woman can no longer bear children and is no longer needed by those whom she has borne.

Traditionally, women who have devoted their attention to their families and have not worked outside the home have felt lost and without purpose at this point. We do not have sufficient evidence to know what middle age and mid-career issues mean for women in management. This means in management development activities there should be at least two basic directions.

First, there should be opportunities for women who have had families, now grown and gone, to talk together about that loss and change in their lives. They should also have the opportunity to talk about the meaning of menopause to them. Sometimes in large organizations members of the medical staff can help. There are, of course, many working women who are not married, but who would have preferred to marry and to have families. With the approach of mid-life and certainly menopause, such women lose their opportunity to have children, often a great disappointment and regret. They, too, should have an opportunity to talk about those losses and to evolve ways of compensating for them. Some will do so in voluntary work in children's agencies; some may find gratification in the counseling of the mentor role.

The second direction should be opportunities for women to talk together about mid-life and mid-career issues with respect to their working and managerial roles. In such discussions they can specify their concerns and help organize for coping with them. Those kinds of meetings should also yield information for people in management development and personnel to evolve more specific programs. Women will need the same kind of pre-retirement planning as is necessary for men. No doubt in time to come, women who have lifelong working careers will also be concerned about alternative careers in mid-life.

Through the generative stage the central thrust of management development should be around teaching managers leadership roles. Organizations are no longer so easily held together by hierarchical bureaucracy or compulsion, nor are people so easily motivated by money alone or fear of loss of job. Cohesion in an organization, as indicated earlier, must be built around the leadership.

The leadership role should be clearly distinguished from management and from administration. Administration historically has meant keeping the wheels of the bureaucracy functioning well. Management is the same kind of function at a higher level, which often may involve moving the boxes or structures of a hierarchy. It also includes the introduction of management sciences. Leadership, however, gives a central thrust to the adaptive efforts of the organization, and that in turn requires that the energies of people be mobilized so that the collective energy of the organization may be available for the adaptation of the whole. Characteristically, too much energy is tied up in maintaining the informal structure in the face of a formal one, in being highly self-protective, in avoiding blame. Competitive rivalry within the organization and passive resistance to authority are set up.

Developmental Programs for the Integrity Phase. Most management development activity stops before the stage of integrity, beginning about fifty-five. It should not. Many managers and executives at that age will continue to hold responsible positions for at least ten more years. Most need personal refreshment and professional updating. Some will have become terribly obsolete, particularly in their understanding of the motivation of the young people new to management ranks. In my experience there is a two-generation gap among managers and executives in the understanding of motivation: between the top and the middle, and between the middle and bottom, but usually along age lines. Older managers, too, have considerable difficulty understanding the new ways brought in by younger executives who have risen to power over them and who perceive the world differently. Sometimes they feel betrayed by managements which have passed over them. Often they are frightened at the prospect of retirement; few know what to do constructively in that period.

Management development activities for people in this stage should be based on the opportunity to talk about all these feelings in groups. Only if these issues are discussed, the changes mourned, and new adaptive modes worked out can people learn further. One of the major psychological issues at this point is to come to terms with the ego ideal. It becomes painfully clear that one's life is nearly spent, that he cannot recover any part of it or do things differently, that he must accept whatever course he has taken and whatever outcome it has produced. If he can come to terms with his ego ideal, then he can integrate his life experiences. If not, then he will continue to despair.

Such discussion might give rise to a number of possibilities. Older managers might well be trained for long-range planning. Older persons are in an excellent position to integrate the new with the old, thereby not losing the character of the organization in planning change. They are more likely to be able to look at long-run consequences, rather than the projected short-term results that are being pressed so hard by younger managers who want to establish their records. Older managers also serve well as confidants, mentors, and guides for the new—providing they learn to listen and counsel. Therefore much of management development can be concentrated on this understanding and counseling.

A long sabbatical of several months, focused on thinking and planning for retirement or an alternative career, would be a good follow-up to individual counseling and group discussion of retirement planning and prospects.

The older a person becomes and the longer he is in an organization, necessarily the more dependent he is on that organization. Therefore older managers need more frequent and more direct demonstrations that they are held in esteem. They should have the opportunity for frequent meetings with higher-level executives in which that esteem and regard can be communicated by providing them with information, entertaining their questions, and hearing their concerns. Given rapid organizational change, they will need reassurance that their contributions have indeed been important and will not be sacrificed on the altar of expediency. Both paranoid and depressive anxieties can thus be lowered. In short, management development activities at this point in time should be geared to combating isolation and obsolescence, establishing greater equanimity, confirming worth, looking to the future, and consolidating a lifetime experience with a sense of having had an effect as an individual.

Implications for Compensation and Personnel Evaluation

Historically managements have assumed that man is motivated by money and seeks to attain it or avoid losing it. While there is a significant element of truth in this assumption, it is not today as dominant a motivator of people, as earlier discussion of personality development and its implications has already demonstrated, unless they are indeed hungry and must be concerned primarily with survival.

Fostering Relatedness. When money is used as a motivator in carrot-and-stick fashion, inevitably people will seek to minimize the stick behind and maximize the carrot in front. Feeling manipulated, they will inevitably manipulate back, to preserve their self-esteem, thus leading to unionization, featherbedding, and other ways of exerting control over their working environments. When people are pitted against each other competitively, they will establish norms of productivity which protect their self-images. When units are pitted against each other, they will often resort to distorted reporting, empire building, protectionism, and similar self-centered efforts to support their self-esteem. The more rigid the control systems and the more focused the appraisal system, the more likely people are to concentrate on those activities that will make them look good.

Such behavior breeds mistrust, inhibits cooperation, and maximizes the self-centeredness of the individual or of the group at the expense of the effectiveness of the whole operation. Short-term gain is maximized at the cost of long-run adaptive perpetuation. Therefore, careful attention must be given to compensation and appraisal practices. In keeping with this theory, compensation and appraisal should foster the individual's relatedness to other individuals and to the organization as a whole as well as the effectiveness with which the individual's and the organization's work is accomplished.

Compensation and appraisal should also support modes through which the individual is able to have some effect on his own fate by having an effect on the organization. Only by doing so can he attain that maturity which also carries with it the sense of responsibility for the organization's fate. This requires a three-step process: goal setting, appraisal, and compensation.

Goals and Objectives. The mutual process of setting goals and objectives for the organization's tasks and occupational roles is the crucial base for individual and organizational performance. While many companies give considerable lip service to management by objectives and many others try to practice management by objectives (MBO), more often than not, this process is simply another carrot-and-stick manipulative effort.

The reason is that although people are told that they have opportunities to set their own objectives, in fact they merely are given a limited range of choices within those established by their superiors and often must modify their own objectives to meet the expectations of management. The objectives they have defined may not be truly theirs, but they are nevertheless compelled to put their own cheese (goals) at the end of the maze. If they do not run the maze well enough to get the cheese, they are then criticized for not meeting their own objectives. I would have no objection to people being told what they are being paid for and the conditions of promotion. I object to their being manipulated into pretending those objectives are necessarily theirs or that they have set them.

A second reason that management by objectives is frequently hollow is that in many instances subordinates do not have enough information to set their own goals. Few know the details of the structures above them, even fewer are aware of political implications, and still fewer know the requirements and demands their superiors have to meet. In the absence of formal knowledge about the dimensions of the career terrain they are to traverse, their objectives can only be shots in the dark.

For an MBO program to be truly effective it should begin with the objectives of the individual. That is, what is his ego ideal? Where would he like to go? How has that aspiration changed over time? These and similar issues need to be discussed between superior and subordinate and to be relayed to higher management as accurately as possible. Once the individual's objectives have been laid out (this is no easy task and cannot be done unless there is an atmosphere of trust), then it becomes possible to juxtapose the individual's objectives and the organization's objectives and to ascertain the degree to which both can be met in the same activity. If they cannot be, then, of course, the individual must decide what he wants to do. However, if they can be, then the superior and the subordinate should work out ways of doing so with reasonable objectives that meet both goals.

Appraisal. Such a system, in turn, calls for appraisal. Most appraisal in organizations is both superficial and downward. Much of it is inadequate and inaccurate because of the guilt aroused in managers who unconsciously feel that to appraise someone negatively is to destroy him. Thus, many people spend many years thinking they are doing well when in fact they are not and ultimately must be discharged at a time when they are no longer so readily able to find alternative roles in the marketplace.[34]

Appraisal fails also because most objectives are stated in terms of the outcomes of the performance being evaluated rather than in terms of the behavior expected in the process of obtaining those outcomes.[35] Appraisal forms therefore tend to become mechanical checklists. Superiors dislike appraising periodically because often they see no relationship between the items on the form and the behavior of the person, and because they lack the documentation to support their judgment. Furthermore, people may attain objectives but behave in ways which are unacceptable to superiors.

Job descriptions and goals should be stated in behavioral terms: What is the person to do in the job and *how* is he to do it? What different behaviors are required in different facets of the job? What nuances of behavior make a significant difference?

What political climate must be taken into account? Such specificity is more realistic than mere statement of responsibilities and outcomes expected.

In addition, the superior should describe on paper in a paragraph or so both the positive and negative behavior of the subordinate each time an incident occurs which is of sufficient importance to be noted. Simultaneously he should tell the subordinate and give him a copy. Thus, the superior will be able to document his judgment at appraisal time, and the subordinate will have no surprises. This critical incident method is especially important in a climate of litigation, particularly about alleged discrimination. It is also important in an organization where managers are rotated rapidly. New managers are often asked to appraise subordinates they have known only briefly. Subordinates who have had several managers in a short period of time often feel they must prove themselves to each. Documented behavior helps both superior and subordinate cope with their strangeness to each other. Also, such specific feedback on behavior makes it clearer to the person what changes in behavior are required of him than do the gross generalizations of most performance appraisals.

A personnel folder containing a number of descriptions of actual behavior becomes an important basis for selection and assignment. Only from such a behavioral basis can adequate inferences be made about the person's characteristic mode of handling affection, aggression, and dependency and the nature of his ego ideal.

An appraisal system should be a three-way mechanism. It should include frequent downward appraisal in the form of critical incidents and summarizing meetings so the subordinate always knows where he stands. This tends to minimize the paranoid and depressive anxieties and to confirm the behavior of the subordinate in the sense that he is experiencing frequent approval for what he is doing or getting information to help him redirect his efforts. Confirmation is necessary because, given the kinds of ego ideals and self-images that most of us have, and therefore the wide gaps between them, we are likely to be harshly self-critical and to think we are doing less well than literally we are. Such negative feelings about oneself maximize anxiety and protective efforts and drain energy which otherwise might go into task performance. Lowered self-image also exacerbates rivalry and fear that others may be placed ahead of one. However, downward appraisal is only one dimension of a comprehensive appraisal process. The superior cannot know how well he is doing with respect to developing the subordinate, for which he is responsible, unless he can hear from the subordinate his feelings and experiences about their relationship. So there should always be an upward appraisal in which the subordinate can report to a superior how he feels his superior is doing with respect to his leadership role. He may speak from firsthand experience about how well he thinks he is developing, the kinds of experiences he thinks he needs, how his superior may get in his way, the kind of support he is getting, and so on. Upward appraisals should be put in writing, as should downward appraisals, and a copy should go to the superior's superior in order to protect the subordinate. One of the major advantages of following such a procedure is that there begins to be built in the superior's file a record of his effectiveness as a developer of people. As a result, for the first time there would be a means of being able to pay him for the effectiveness of his developmental activity.

Upward appraisal is easier said than done. Even under the best of circumstances, it is difficult to get subordinates to evaluate their superiors. One useful method is for the superior to ask his subordinates to define the criteria by which they would appraise his job. To do so might take weekly meetings over a period of several months. By the time the criteria have been defined, they are more comfortable talking about his performance. He can then ask them to appraise him.

Finally, there should be a group appraisal process. By this I mean that people who work together, either under the same superior or reporting to different superiors, should set group goals for themselves and evaluate how well they have done at whatever periods of time are appropriate. The person to whom they report their collective work should enter his own appraisal in the folder of each group member.

Compensation. To complement the three-way appraisal procedure there should be a three-way compensation system. That is, first people should be paid whatever they are worth in the marketplace. In addition, they should receive a pro-rata share of the profitability which reflects the effectiveness of the group of which they are a part and on which they can have an effect. Further, they should have a pro-rata share of the profitability which reflects the effectiveness of the organization. The organization may be a single plant, or it may be a component of a plant. Whatever it is should be limited to that part of a company over which the employee can exert some influence and on which his thoughts, feelings, and behavior have some effect. Ideally compensation should be as direct a feedback on performance as possible and an information device which helps the employee meet his ego ideal requirements rather than a method of reward and punishment.

The actual mode of compensation may vary with different groups of people, depending on their value systems, to be discussed later. Some may want cash, others deferred benefits, still others greater developmental opportunities or other forms of recognition. Elliott Jaques argues for a method of compensation based on the "time span of responsibility."[36] By that method the longer a person goes without being supervised, the more he is paid. His concept merits serious consideration, based as it is on the superego.

The criteria by which the effectiveness of the group and the organization are to be measured may be defined by negotiation between people who are in that group or organization and the management. Those criteria should be subject to appropriate change through continuous legislative effort on the part of both partners. Compensation should always be an index of adaptive effectiveness. Too often bonuses have no relationship to the task at hand. Profit-sharing usually has little to do with how well an employee has done his job and more often has to do with whether top management has made extraordinary expenditures. Incentives usually lead to maximizing self-centeredness. None of these reward-punishment types of compensation contributes to cohesiveness of identification or effectiveness of the organization. None fosters better relationships among people and between people and the organization.

There are many complications to evolving a compensation system. Compensation is often constrained by labor-management agreements, industrywide standards and practices, minimum wage laws, and so on. Various plans for compensating people have been evolved which have returned to participants a share of the savings of cutting costs, or of overall profitability. The concept I have outlined above is not intended to be merely another simple profit-sharing activity or a universal solution to replace previous universal solutions which have not worked well. Rather it is an effort to respond to the need to relate compensation as directly to performance as is possible, so that it becomes automatic feedback. Such an effort should allow for varying individual competences and needs and should support group formation and effectiveness and identification with the outcome of performance for the whole organization. It should also be supported by managerial processes through which people can meet together to look at what they are doing and to effect those changes in structure and process which would allow it to be done better. Finally, compensation must be supported by a comprehensive appraisal process. Without this three-dimensional conception, compensation is likely to be unrelated to either behavior or outcome, except in the most general way, and motivation continues to be heavily reward-punishment oriented.

Implications for Selection and Assignment

Ideally, selection and assignment is a process of fitting and refitting as both persons and tasks change over time. The process should be based on a configuration of the interaction of a number of different forces which operate continuously. Effective processes of selection and placement facilitate the opportunity for a person to master his work and integrate it as a creative and constructive part of his personality. Among these forces are: (1) crisis-specific psychological needs; (2) values and value-system behaviors; (3) need-level requirements; (4) a person's career stage; (5) age-specific proclivities; (6) stage-specific psychological tasks; and (7) changing organizational adaptive patterns.

I indicated earlier that people are always engaged in maintaining their psychological equilibria, and therefore the work they choose to do is instrumental in that effort. I spoke of defining occupational roles according to the manner in which they permit a person to attain and give affection, to cope with his aggressive impulses and dependency needs, and to meet the demands of his ego ideal. Once technical proficiency is established, selection then becomes largely a matter of assessing with the individual his preferred mode of handling these drives and self-demands at the particular life stage in which he finds himself. Earlier in this chapter I spoke of career stages, age-specific proclivities, and stage-specific psychological tasks.

Crisis-Specific Psychological Needs. Career stages and age-specific psychological tasks interrelate to give rise to crisis-specific psychological needs. By crisis-specific, I refer to crises of normal development. Some are more environmentally determined, others are more a product of internal psychological processes. For example, for many young people there is a crisis experience around the issue of occupational choice. For both men and women, becoming parents may accentuate this issue. Certainly it accentuates the problem of accepting the dependency of others on them. For the first time they are responsible for the life of someone other than themselves. This may have import with respect to the additional burden of accepting the dependency of those whom they must supervise, or with organizational demands which come in conflict with parental responsibilities. Many have a need at this point to understand the nature of the crisis they are experiencing, to find support in coping with it, and to develop avenues of action through which it might be resolved.

Tapping the Ego Ideal. Since the ego ideal is the personal road map which must be unfolded, one should begin there. The ego ideal may be tapped in many ways. None of them, however, provides more than a partial glimpse because much of the ego ideal is unconscious. For example, considering the importance of early influences on occupational choice, it would be important to know what is the earliest memory a man has about doing something which pleased his mother or a woman her father. Chances are such behavior is represented in his or her contemporary striving. It would also be important to know what his father's (her mother's) values were, what was important to him, for these values are likely to be represented in the present ego ideal. A person can list each of the life and career choices he has made, such as a choice between one school subject and another, between one course and another, between one job and another. While these may appear to be random, retrospective examination will disclose that there is a pattern to those choices. The pattern represents the unfolding ego ideal, and its projection is the psychological road map which the person is following. Another mode of tapping the ego ideal is to learn who were a person's early models: who were his (her) heroes and who were his (her) mentors? Still another is to ask the person to recount those few peak experiences in his (her) lifetime when he was extremely gratified with himself, when he felt "on top of the world." In those vignettes lie the kernel of the ego ideal.

Another way of looking at the ego ideal issue for groups of people is to assess the expectations people have about how much they want their ministration, maturation, and mastery needs to be met in an organization and the degree to which they feel they are. This can be done by questionnaire.[37] Those who are employed in an organization which provides long-term stability but slow advancement are likely to have more powerful ministration needs and require greater dependency gratification. Those in an organization which provides a wide range of growth and movement for the acquisition of competence and skill probably have high maturation needs. An organization which renders professional service is likely to provide the context for meeting mastery needs.

Values. Basically, the issue is values. Values are fundamental beliefs which are developed out of earliest identifications with the parents and other power figures or models. They are all those ideas, ideals, concepts, and precepts which an individual holds dear. Values give rise to attitudes, and attitudes in turn to the way one perceives or interprets the world around him, including his own relationship to that world. They determine what a person appreciates or disdains and who he will willingly love or die for. Values are deeply held and unconsciously ingrained; therefore they are significant components of the ego ideal and the self-image. For example, the value placed on human life reinforced by a heavy religious tradition, captured in the commandment, "Thou shalt not kill," is so powerful that even in military combat many people cannot fire their rifles in self-defense. Some people in hunting animals experience "buck fever," tremors of such proportion that they cannot fire their weapons. These are extreme illustrations of what is meant by values.

We see values reflected in integrity on the part of some people, or the feeling on the part of others that it is acceptable to exploit people if they are not members of an ingroup, ethnic group, or subculture. For some groups education is highly valued and for others it is looked upon with disdain, with the phrase "longhair." Some independent artisans, like carpenters and plumbers, place a high value on independence and have contempt for those who must work in organizations where somebody else dictates their occupational behavior. In many cultures masculinity is highly valued, and certain characteristics are considered indicative of masculinity. In our culture it is victorious competition, whether in athletics or business. In other cultures it may have to do with the number of wives a man can afford. In still others, the important value for a man is the responsibility he assumes for the members of his extended family.

Values may have to do with work, religion, recreation, interpersonal relationships, or any other crucial element of life. They often cluster together. A person for whom religious precepts are highly important will probably also value interpersonal relationships and service to others. This clustering makes it possible to evolve scales of values, which is one mode of measuring values.

The Allport-Vernon Scale of Values is the most widely known of these.[38] Such a scale reflects peoples' interests in commercial, aesthetic, scientific, artistic, or similar directions, and with what

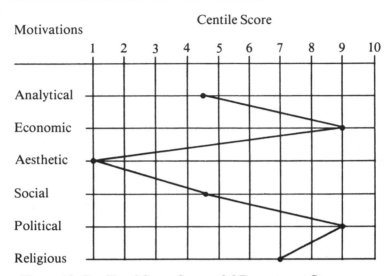

**Figure 10. Profile of Some Successful Department Store
Managers: Allport-Vernon-Lindzey Value Scores**

degrees of intensity and in what combination. The use of such a
scale results in a profile which may then be compared with the
values required by the task to be done. The successful operation
of a retail store would require a person who valued commercial
interests, for example. Vocational interest tests and aptitude
measures often help round out some of the picture. However,
the latter tend to be gross, general devices which ask people their
preferences, comparing one potential kind of activity with another and breaking down those wishes into the components I
have enunciated here.

Value System Behavior. A new value system technique has been
evolved by M. Scott Myers, Charles Hughes, and Vincent S.
Flowers, building on a theory of Clare C. Graves.[39] This is a
seven-value system which incorporates a level of thinking (concrete or abstract), level of initiative, level of dependency, level of

socialization, level of reflection about oneself and one's career goals. These in some respects parallel stages of psychosexual development. Determining these levels among employees makes it possible to address different groups of employees differently. Employee communications, job design, management systems and procedures, compensation, and growth opportunities have to be fitted to people who differ on these values or they will be unable to hear the communications, the jobs will be ungratifying, the systems and procedures will make no sense, and offers of growth may not fit the people. The seven value systems are:

(1) Reactive, that is, primitive response to physiological needs.

(2) Tribalistic, valuing easy work, friendly people, fair play, and a good boss. Money and supervisory direction are important.

(3) Egocentric, which emphasizes good pay and freedom from being tied down.

(4) Conformist, which values job security, rules, and fairness.

(5) Manipulative, in which there is variety of work, some free-wheeling activity, and pay and bonuses based on results. Mastery, power, and political manipulation are important considerations.

(6) Sociocentric, where friendly relationships, doing what one likes to do and working with others to a common goal are important. Material issues are secondary to social contributions.

(7) Existential, in which goals and problems are more important than money, prestige, or methodology. The preference here is for continuing challenge, imagination, and initiative.

Determining by questionnaire which of the value systems various people hold makes it possible to differentiate employee communications, job design, management systems and procedures, and growth opportunities which fit the needs of people who hold these diverse value structures. This is important groundwork for differentiation and refinement of occupational roles and career paths. The authors are attempting to specify the intensity and degree to which various kinds of career issues, age- and stage-specific issues and crises will affect one or another group of people.

Changing Psychological Needs. The value system conception ties in nicely with Maslow's concept of hierarchy of needs, which is another way of differentiating occupational role according to the need level of the employee. Maslow classified human needs on five levels, each becoming pressing as the preceding ones were satisfied.[40] In ascending order these are: physiological needs, safety needs, needs for belonging and love, needs for esteem, and needs for self-actualization. Such needs presumably would cut across the developmental pattern which I outlined earlier in the form of career stages, age-specific proclivities, stage-specific psychological tasks, and crisis-specific psychological needs. While the Maslow concept applies across the board, and complements the value system idea, the latter suggests that various people become fixed at different points. The Maslow conception suggests the possibility of raising the need levels for people who are fixated at various points and thereby, presumably, freeing them and the organization for more adaptive efforts. While the Myers, Hughes, and Flowers conception would seem to speak for organizing work around groups differentiated according to values, Maslow points to directions in which movement might take place. For example, conceivably a manager who holds value system (5) manipulative, might change as a result of experiences in the middle-age crisis to a value system (6) sociocentric, or a value system (7) existential. In fact, if such movement were possible and desired by an individual, a company could facilitate his movement in that direction by redefining occupational roles which would allow such movement to take place.

Values, value system behavior, and need level requirements are additional orienting points for looking into the ego ideal. In the process of performance appraisal, career counseling, and other discussions about one's work and life plans, as a person seeks to define what he or she wants of work and an organization, the ego ideal becomes increasingly refined in the person's mind. This will help him and the organization make more appropriate career and placement decisions.

At the level of entry to an organization, these conceptions may be used as follows:

> Irwin Mollens, a young man fresh from business school, was being interviewed for a responsible overseas managerial assignment in a situation which would require that he operate pretty much alone. The country in which the assignment was located was hostile to Americans and especially hostile to businessmen. The new job required considerable political finesse and even more patience, forbearance, and persistence. In the course of the interview with his prospective employers Mr. Mollens was asked in what extracurricular activities he had participated as an undergraduate. He replied that he had been in the glee club and on the swimming team. He was then asked to what campus clubs he had belonged and what offices he had held as an undergraduate. He said that he had not held any campus offices and had belonged to very few clubs. His experience before returning to business school involved being an executive assistant to a major executive of a widely known company. In that role he was truly an assistant and carried out no major or independent responsibilities himself. He enjoyed the job, which involved putting together various kinds of reports, gathering information, and in other ways being helpful to his boss. In talking about the prospective job, he mentioned that he had read a newspaper interview with an American executive who had departed in angry frustration from the country to which he would be assigned. When asked what he would do under similar circumstances, he said he would do the same thing.

Here we see a man who has not yet clarified for himself his own ego ideal strivings nor taken advantage of his moratorium opportunity to juxtapose his own wishes and needs with those of the prospective work environment. Mr. Mollens has never been in an independent activity; his interests have been heavily oral and certainly not individually competitive. He has not previously sought power or managerial achievement. His interests would be considered more aesthetic and artistic than commercial. Probably he would be close to a value system (6), sociocentric, where friendly relationships, doing what one likes to do and working toward a common goal are important. In the situation which Mr. Mollens was considering, there would have been little opportunity for supervisory support, for modeling himself on others, for discussing crises of the work, or for increasing capacities and experiences by working with others who were more experienced than he. This point in his life was perhaps a time when he might have been creative, and he needed an organization and an environment which would involve him in finding out what he could do. Mr. Mollens had apparently not been very spontaneously creative. He seemed to handle his affectional needs by investing that drive in his work; his aggression equally so. He did not relate himself easily and flexibly to other people, which would have enabled him to sell himself or to negotiate acceptable relationships under difficult circumstances. He had always been in situations where somebody else had assumed direction, and he depended on them for that kind of leadership. He was not a good candidate for the role which he sought.

Beyond the entry level are people who have begun to get organizational experience. They must now begin to make choices or to consolidate themselves around a choice they have made. The following two examples are illustrative.

Ernest Kimball, twenty-five, had majored in economics and said that he did so because he thought that seemed to be the most practical thing to do. At the same time his greatest gratification in college came from his work in art. After he graduated he worked for a short time in marketing activities but yearned to go back to graduate school. He was torn between business and architecture. A brief stint working for an architect had given him a feeling for that professional activity. Although he was enamored of being a professional, he did not want to spend the rest of his life at a drawing board. Rather he felt he would like to develop communities that would be good for people. As we examined his wishes and views, it became apparent that while Mr. Kimball liked to work with other people in close team collaboration and handled his wish to love and be loved by this kind of interdependence, he also wanted to retain enough independence to develop his own imaginative creativity. He handled his aggression by close attention to tasks at hand, by organizing what he had to do, by accomplishing appropriate tasks, and by investing himself in both his academic work and the process of earning a livelihood. He did not want to work under direct, continued supervision, nor could he see spending all of his time merely drawing plans. Mr. Kimball had to act, to do, to acquire power in the process of becoming a business success and doing social good. As it turned out, his foster father was a prominent business executive and the son in many ways wished to emulate the father but still wanted greater personal freedom. The father was in an industry which at that time was being criticized for its disregard for environmental considerations. The son did not want to be so criticized. In fact, it would seem that there was a wish on his part to make up for that kind of criticism and to do social good. He had been accepted for an architectural program and also for a business school program. He felt that he needed both to prepare for the career he wanted. As he saw it, it seemed to be an either/or process. However, in the course of discussion, it became clear that he did not have to choose between the two. He could take both and they could complement each other. He then had to struggle with the problem of which should come first, business or architecture. After some extended discussion, it became apparent that, given the kind of creativity he wanted to develop in architecture and land development, he would be far better off to take architecture first, because his major creativity would come in the period before he was thirty-five. If he were to take a business course first and then architecture, he would fail to take advantage of that stage in his development when he was most creative. Thus, by applying the concepts we have already discussed in terms of the present age-stage context, he could make a rational career decision.

Similarly, Donna Lerner, a thirty-year-old single woman who had attained an excellent reputation as a teacher, found herself faced with a need to decide among a range of career alternatives. She had been reared in a very close and warm family where she was held in high regard by both parents. She had been everybody's favorite as a child, a charming girl who made friends easily and for whom, now as an adult, all kinds of people had great admiration and affection. As a consequence, Ms. Lerner had had great success in her chosen professional role, and that role also met the ego ideal demands on which a traditional, Protestant, midwestern American background placed heavy emphasis. She had handled affection in a mature way, both getting and giving affection in the course of her teaching experiences and her multiple professional and social relationships. She had not married, presumably having been preoccupied with the gratifications of her career and her achievement. The achievement in turn was fostered by the support and esteem of both her parents, particularly her father, who encouraged her to do whatever she wanted to do. She modulated her aggression and directed it appropriately into helping others learn and into being a model for them. Now at thirty, however, Ms. Lerner found herself facing a need to enhance her competence and skill because she felt that there was much more to her field that she could learn and become competent in. The alternatives, then, were to continue doing what she was already doing, at which she was quite proficient, or to go back to school to acquire greater skill. She had no great yen for paper credentials or more routine academic experiences. She felt that there were limits to what she could learn in most academic settings about the subject matter in which she was a specialist. She did not want to be taken out of the classroom situation and, as a byproduct of advanced learning, directed toward research or administration. Both of these directions would have conflicted with her characteristic modes of handling her drives. In addition, she could gratify her dependency needs by directly meeting the appropriate dependency needs of her students. That, too, would be missing if she were to go into research and administration, although in the latter situation she would have more people dependent on her in a more indirect way. To complicate matters, at her stage of development, the state of intimacy, she had not yet married and had children, both of which she wanted very much. Without a husband and without children, Ms. Lerner saw herself as incomplete. She had only a limited number of years during which to have a family. Each passing year narrowed the range of opportunity. The crucial issue in this instance was a redefinition of her ego ideal according to the stage in which she now found herself. In her case it was extremely helpful for her to discuss those issues with a professional counselor. Others might not need to do so unless they found themselves in similarly severe conflict over making such choices. She chose to stay in her present work, enhancing her skills with short courses, and continuing to be in contact with a wide range of people, including eligible men.

I have presented both of these from the point of view of the persons themselves. It might just as well have been from the point of view of a superior, or somebody in a personnel department who was concerned with selecting people for given positions or promoting people to new responsibilities. By assessing the needs of the individual with that person, examining the range of alternatives in keeping with that person's preferred mode of adaptation and that person's needs at a given time, the superior or personnel executive could juxtapose the requirements of the task against those of the individual and make more reasonable choices about placement.

For example, in the first case, if the issue were a placement issue within a company, Ernest Kimball should have been directed toward an area where he would have opportunity to use his creative imagination and at the same time begin to acquire those managerial skills which, complementing the imaginative development, might enable him to take increasing managerial responsibility as he aged.

In the second instance, to have assumed that Donna Lerner would have been a good administrator because she was such an excellent teacher and liked by everybody would have failed to take into account some of the conflicts she was experiencing because of the particular stage at which she found herself and the requirements of her ego ideal. Though she might have given a good account of herself as an administrator, the chances are she would have been more mechanical in that role than as a teacher and would have experienced increasing frustration in it as the time span during which she could bear children narrowed. The same might have been true if she were in a business organization and were being asked to take on more managerial or executive responsibility.

Observe that in the first adult stage there is a good deal of self-preoccupation, interest in career development and in attaining a range of experience to prepare for continuing advancement or achievement and, particularly in the case of the woman, in establishing a family. At the same time, both persons are driven to demonstrate their own competence, to show themselves what they can do in a creative fashion.

Seen from the point of view of career patterns, we observe that both persons are in an early phase.[41] They are still casting about for direction, to a certain extent for a sense of purpose, and for a more refined area of specialization while building a range of experiences out of which to develop a general career pattern. Notice that both persons have tried themselves out, have sampled working relationships, and have developed skills and reputations.

If either of these persons had been in a formal career development or management development program in an organization, he would have had the opportunity to view the whole of the organization before undertaking to work in one or another area. He would also have had the opportunity to test himself, to show what he can do, to develop a sense of competence, usefulness, and value.

In one major organization the chief executive officer makes it a point to draw from the pool of young managerial talent a new young person each year to serve as his executive assistant. In a role much like that of law clerk to a Supreme Court justice, the young person gets a view of the chief executive's job, the multiple conflicting forces to be dealt with, and a perspective on the role behavior of an executive. When he returns to a line operation for the further development of skills and competence, his work is then undertaken against an understanding of the full organization, its political structure, its demands on executive role performance, and an appreciation of the socioeconomic context in which the organization operates. Thus, such a person is in a more realistic position to evolve the development of his career, skills, competences, and life direction.

In both examples, one can observe that the age range of these young people is a time of questioning, juxtaposing academic experiences with those of the real world, examining parental values not as a student but as a mature adult, earning a livelihood, and warily making choices. This suggests that it is unwise to pressure young people to make formal choices or to force them into sticking with an organization. Rather it might be better to view this period as one of mutual examination—occupational dating, so to speak. This kind of exploration is an age-specific proclivity.

People also have stage-specific psychological tasks. There are psychological tendencies which have a peak at one stage of development and indeed constitute great internal pressures at that time. In these two cases it is easy to observe that the stage of intimacy is also a period during which still-maturing people more easily deny their underlying dependency needs, for they see themselves as more instrumental than older or younger people. That is, they are more active, support themselves and often others, and they have not yet arrived at the point where they are declining physically. Taken together these forces compel an action orientation.

At this point young people need a great deal of supportive supervision which will enable them to act creatively while being protected from the rest of the organization. Simultaneously they should have impulsive and poorly thought-through activities reasonably guided and controlled, so as to be productive. Such supervision will have to deal with feelings of intense rivalry, the residues of attempting to establish close adult interpersonal relationships of an enduring kind.

Mid-Life: Age and Career. Although one may have selected people carefully for their initial jobs in the organization and placed them according to their needs, the dynamic quality of life makes it impossible to think of static positions. The configuration of all of these forces may also be seen vividly in mid-career and middle age.

In mid-career, one presumably has established an occupational reputation and acquired competence and skills. Mid-career is frequently a time of powerful identification with the organization in which one works or with the profession one practices. It is a time in which one acts on behalf of the organization and represents it both to subordinates and to its various publics. It is the mature action phase of career, one which is closest to the parental role in the family. As we shall see in both of the cases described next, work in this period ideally involves leadership and supervisory activities, responsibility for other people, responsibility for representing the organization and acting on its behalf in the sense of mature partnership with the organization.

The mid-life period is the time when a person reorganizes his thinking about himself. Taking into account his mortality, he restructures his value system, changes emphases in his life activity, and copes with the loss of his growing family. He comes to terms with the limitations of his aspirations prescribed by time, experience, life station, and opportunity.[42] The task in middle age, therefore, is to free oneself from self-centered self-indulgence and competitiveness and become instrumental in rearing others.

With the declining average age at which men and women become company presidents, many more people will know earlier in their lives that they are no longer competitive for higher management positions. Ideally, many should make the shift from a playing role to a coaching role. The psychological work of this period is not only to make this shift, but to accept oneself in the new role.

Todd Adams, in his early forties, had attained a line vice presidency in a large distribution organization. He came from a religious family which placed a heavy emphasis on social responsibility, but equal emphasis on business success. He had done well as an executive in the organization in which he was employed and had been in that organization an occupational lifetime. He was a competitive person whose aggression was well channeled into his successful business career. Having established himself, now moving into the generative period, Mr. Adams became increasingly concerned with the development of other people, especially with competent replacements for himself and other executives in his age range. He saw the need for a vital, lively, flexible group of young people who could continue the expansion of the organization in novel ways required for the increasing competition they faced. His concern with development of others led him to become increasingly preoccupied with the barriers to that development which he saw in a rigid organizational structure that was continually being tightened with new systems for measurement. He began to protest the rigidities of these systems and to point out their costs in terms of developing a new managerial cadre. His protests fell on deaf ears. Facing increasing pressure from his ego ideal and being unable to have an effect on the organization which would help him meet these new stage-specific requirements, Mr. Adams ultimately resigned to devote his efforts to public service.

By her mid-forties, Rita McGrath had attained a personnel vice presidency. Reviewing her career and her present function in middle age, she decided that her gratifications had come primarily from direct relationships with people, and her most effective work had come when she could channel her aggression into helping people solve problems, pursue their own career goals more actively, and move toward their own more effective attainments. In her personnel VP role, she had been largely responsible for techniques, methods, systems, and procedures. The development of these activities fitted her stage in life and her wish to attain high position. Having attained that and now having reached middle age, she was less contented with that type of work. As a consequence, reviewing where she stood and the demands of her ego ideal, she decided to build on some of her early psychological training. While still in her official role, she enrolled in courses in counseling and psychotherapy. With the completion of her formal training, she began to conduct a private practice after working hours. Shortly thereafter, she resigned her job in the company to undertake a full time independent career as a counselor and psychotherapist, which was more in keeping with her stage in life.

In both of these instances, people important to the company, who had made significant contributions, were compelled to leave. Had the respective higher managements sensed their stage-specific requirements as well as the implications of what they were doing, these two people might have been supported within the organization. Mr. Adams might well have been put in charge of a task force to review and modify those aspects of the organization which were being destructive to the development of a replacement cadre. Ms. McGrath might well have been put in a position of counselor to higher-level management, a position which she could have filled since she was trusted by higher-level management. However, nobody thought to ask her about where she wanted to go and what she wanted to do with herself.

As we have seen from both these cases, in the second stage of adult development, that of generativity, people become more interested in the development of others. Both are going through the middle-age crisis and need time to think and reflect, take stock, make new choices in keeping with their new value emphases. They are psychologically ready to be crucial cords of communication and cohesion in organizations as developers of others, absorbers of organizational shocks and pressures, and persons of stability within the organization. They are likely to be less and less imaginatively capable except as they expand their earlier repertoire. They have begun to think of the time they have left in their lives and how to use it best, and there is, therefore, likely to be a shift in values and in emphasis which makes them less competitive and more content with what they have achieved for themselves.

As indicated earlier, Daniel Levinson has called attention to the crisis experience which occurs in the late thirties around "becoming one's own man" or BOOM.[43] When managers begin to assert independence from their mentor, their separation from him, the establishment of themselves as their own men, and the reinvigorated pursuit of their own directions, these thrusts combine to make for an emotional experience of crisis proportions.

Russell Miles, a forty-two-year-old middle manager, fourteen years with his organization, had developed a service program which became important to his organization. This program expanded the reputation of the organization and attracted a significant volume of new business, which also enhanced the organization's reputation. However, though an innovative, creative man of considerable drive, Mr. Miles was not considered a candidate for higher managerial responsibility because he was more technically capable in the avenues on which he was working. He invested himself in his task, and his aggression was focused primarily on program and service development. He gave correspondingly less attention to supporting and developing subordinates or maintaining political relationships within the organizational system. Much of his affection was invested in himself and on the tasks he was doing. That, together with his consequent achievement, did not endear him to his peers. His ego ideal involved unfolding what had now become his new service program and making it a dominant feature of his company's activities as well as an important contributor to profits. Mr. Miles handled his dependency needs by leaning heavily on the development of the service program and the structure around it while acting rather independently with little support from his superiors. The superiors were preoccupied with their own activities and did not provide support. At the end of this extended period of recognition and achievement, which earned him an international reputation, changes in top management and subsequent changes in reporting relationships raised for the middle manager the question of his continued future in and value to the organization. It became apparent to Mr. Miles that he would go no further in the organization and that, despite his achievements, he would be pushed aside and put on a plateau. At this point, he reacted with the characteristic chronological assertion of independence, BOOM. He resigned from the organization and went to another for a period of five years, during which time he simultaneously built up independent activities, which he then ultimately turned to full time as a consultant.

The assertion of independence in Mr. Miles's case was successful because of the step-by-step planning and the content of his work. He resolved the career-stage issues, and those having to do with his specific age proclivities and psychological tasks. He coped well with his crisis-specific psychological needs as well as his value system and need level requirements. Simultaneously, he adapted to the changes in his own organization. He was at the seventh stage in terms of value system behaviors, in which goals and problems were more important to him than money, prestige, and methodology. His preference was for challenge, imagination, and initiative. In terms of the Maslow classification, he was at the level of self-actualization. Obviously, his ego ideal incorporated much of the need to become independent and, to a certain extent, entrepreneurial, while at the same time leaving something professional and conceptual behind.

For many people, a crisis arises in about the fifteenth year of their careers. Often this is connected with the middle-age crisis. Sometimes people feel they have mastered their fields, that there is nothing new and stimulating, and that they must do something else to avoid boredom. These are the people who frequently choose second careers. Those undergoing this crisis need counseling. Particular attention should be given to assessing whether they are depressed. If so, they should have professional guidance before making career choices.

Middle age is a time of beginning physical and intellectual decline. In some occupations, such as that of aircraft controller, one reaches a point when one can no longer be as effective at balancing multiple responsibilities and continuous, heavy amounts of data input as previously. Organic changes which begin to come about in late middle age have special significance for such people as airline pilots, surgeons, and railroad engineers. They may have implications for scientists and technicians who are compelled to deal with increasing complexity at a time of decreasing ability. Such age-specific issues still need to be more clearly understood and correlated with task requirements.

Late Career. In the older age range, Erikson's stage of integrity, people tend to be much more concerned with aging, holding their place, anticipating retirement, and leaving something behind. In this stage one has developed a historical perspective on his own career experiences and on those of the organization. He is no longer competing for position and, therefore, others can more readily turn to him. However, it is also a time of obsolescence, when many managers manage on what they once knew. Therefore, while such people may more conveniently be used and use themselves in a role that calls for counseling, political understanding, taking into account their experience with the past, and giving more careful attention to selection, they should also be required to be involved in anticipating the future. That requirement will sustain their optimism and compel them to continue to learn. Their experience and wisdom can be tapped for long-range thinking in the context of the history and experience of the organization. One would hardly expect an aggressive leadership of organizations or imaginative adaptation or great innovation.

In addition to being a time of consolidation and coming to terms with how one has used one's own life, it is also a time when one's own dependency is increasing because of declining physical and intellectual resources.[44] A person feels less instrumental in the sense of doing what he did in earlier periods. He must deal with gradual detachment from personal activities or from the organization with which he has worked while still making useful contributions to both.

Coming to terms with how one has used his life is a painful psychological task. People who cannot accept their one and only life cycle as something that had to be then despair and fear death. For many people, to leave an organization because of age increases their sense of uselessness and worthlessness. Those who have depended on an organization for a working lifetime feel bereft at a time when they are increasingly dependent because of advancing years. Sometimes they feel that their efforts have been useless if, as they leave, things change so much behind them.

The psychological work of this stage requires preparation for shifting from an authoritative or power role to one of consultation, guidance, and wisdom. Ideally, the work people do at this age should contribute to a sense of wholeness, of career integration. Ideally, too, people at this age should be able to see their integrated life experiences as a platform from which others can start.

The anticipated crisis for a person approaching retirement has chiefly to do with loss of contact with the organization, loss of purpose, and the feeling of being totally forgotten and having little value to others. The retirement experience itself for most is a crisis experience. Few people are adequately prepared for it. Most tend to deny it until the last minute, and little is done in most organizations to provide transitional activities that might be perpetuated ad lib once one has formally left an organization or intensive career activity.

One way to deal with the retirement crisis experience is by helping the prospective retiree establish himself in activities outside the business. Ideally this should be done on a part-time basis beginning, perhaps, at age sixty. If the prospective retiree could undertake an activity on behalf of the organization that would require him to spend more time outside and away from his previous regular duties, that would be even better. Prospective retirees could thus establish themselves away from the organization and gradually separate from it. It is particularly important that they establish themselves, because without membership in the organization they gradually lose their leverage in the community and are left to doing low-level volunteer work, which frequently does not appeal to them. A critical aspect of this experience is the continuous message to the retiree that his work life has indeed been worthwhile, that the company appreciates him, that he still has something to offer, and that he has not wasted his life. Many companies do this by issuing identification cards, allowing continued use of company resources and facilities, continuing to send company publications, and having reunion affairs.

Al Morocco, fifty-six, had built a successful department store chain which subsequently was merged with a larger chain. He had been an outstanding success with novel merchandising methods when he started. His fundamental thrust was based on a three-step definition of his ego ideal. First, he wanted to become highly successful economically so that he could take care of his extended family responsibilities. Then, he wanted to be helpful to his employees and to be liked by them. Finally, he wanted to do something for charities with which he was identified. Mr. Morocco concentrated very heavily on the first and became a wealthy man. After this and after the merger, he found himself subject to systems and controls which were part of the corporate operation, but which had little to do with his successful entrepreneurial way of operating. He found himself less and less at home with methods which he neither understood or could apply. Furthermore, he saw them as adding to the cost of his overhead. His operation, which had been so successful that the parent company wanted it, now turned into a loss situation. Mr. Morocco withdrew more and more from the operation, leaving it to others, but as the operation began to go downhill, he felt a responsibility to justify the reputation of his firm to the parent organization by returning it to its profitability. As he began to push aside the parent organization's systems and controls that had made him so uncomfortable and interfered with his favored ways of relating to people and attacking the marketplace, he discovered that the ideas he was bringing to bear on the contemporary market situation were no longer appropriate. They were the ideas that had been successful twenty-five years before. The marketplace had changed, the neighborhoods in which his stores were located had changed, the sophistication of the customers had changed, and even the nature of his employees had changed. He found himself less successful, though he worked harder and harder. It became apparent to him that he could no longer continue that pace and that he could not go about learning new methods which would be part of his spontaneous way of giving his organization leadership. As a result, after extended discussion Mr. Morocco realized that he had already achieved the first two of his goals. His family was well provided for and he had done all he could to create training programs and other kinds of support for his employees. Now he could freely concentrate on the development of his contribution to the charities with which he was heavily identified. Gradually, with discussion, he was able to give up his attachment to his stores and allow professional management to take over. He shifted his attention to consulting with and advising the leaders of the charity operations with which he had been involved. He managed his personal finances in a way which took only a few hours of his week. The energies which had gone into merchandising and managing now went into establishing the permanence of his charities and their financial stability as well as developing a reputation and a memorial to himself in their achievements. While he regretted leaving his organization, nevertheless Mr. Morocco had to come to terms with himself and to complete the third dimension of his ego ideal, a task which was now paramount. In effect, he was bringing to an integrated close a lifelong thrust of contribution by concentrating on leaving a living memorial behind.

In this example, one sees the pointlessness of trying to manage on what one once knew. One sees also the meaning of Erikson's definition of the phase of integrity. This executive's experience and his interest and the energy which remained could be applied usefully to something which was near and dear to him. He could not apply himself to his charitable activities as he once had to his business, but then that was not necessary. He managed his increasing dependency by accepting the dependency needs of other people and other organizations and maintaining his sense of being instrumental while detaching himself from his organization and his previously dominant activities. Of course, the transition was a painful one. Yet he could look upon the effective way in which he had used his life and the gratifications he had brought to himself and others. While sustaining his contribution, he felt useful and worthwhile as a person. Others in his business and in the charitable work he was doing could build from the contributions he had made and was continuing to make. He acted as a psychological lever in the lives of other people and organizations. He dealt with his crisis wisely by talking about it and seeing it in its full dimensions, including his complex and very mixed feelings. He could perpetuate his new activities until he was no longer physically able to carry them on. His activities outside the business, which he had been developing all along, now became his paramount interest which met the demands of his ego ideal. At the same time, he had moved from value system (5), in which he had been free-wheeling and achievement- and power-oriented, to value system (7), where he had both social problems to cope with and the opportunity to use his imagination and initiative. In Maslow's terms, he was involved at the self-actualization level; in mine, he continued to meet mastery needs.

Career stages vary in different organizations and among different careers. It will be difficult to fix permanent beginning and ending points for them. Simultaneously, as we move further from a blue-collar work force to a white-collar work force, career phases will become more widespread among the population. It will be increasingly necessary to define specific activities within individual career paths and those within career patterns in organizations, and then to gear training and development activities to the enhancement of effectiveness of the individual as he passes through the ages, stages, and phases I have outlined.

Changing Organizational Adaptive Patterns

There is a final dimension to selection and assignment. As organizations change rapidly, there are necessarily significant and often radical role shifts, which usually are quite stressful. Inevitably, tasks and roles are changed and with them the psychological requirements of the people who hold the roles and do the tasks. In many cases organizational changes make roles less psychologically functional for the people who hold them because they no longer support their psychological equilibria. This tends to result in wholesale firing, or in the paralysis of the organization and sometimes in its demise. Often the organizational personality is a coalescence of the collective personalities of the people in the organization, particularly the leadership. But personality collapses when management attempts to substitute a system or procedure—that is, a way of doing things and adapting to the environment—for organizational personality.

This means that in mergers and organizational changes careful attention must be given to the new task requirements, what they now mean for organizational roles, and how people are going to fit into them and adapt to them. Some may need additional support. Others may require an opportunity to deal with lost relationships, competences, and skills by mourning and regrouping. Still others will need greater freedom to meet their own needs for handling affection, aggression, dependency, and their ego ideals. And if merging an organization is like bringing two families together with new stepparents, a great deal of fear and conflict must be anticipated and resolved by role negotiation before the merger can function smoothly.

The fact that this phenomenon has been so widely ignored is reflected in the great difficulty that many organizations have in becoming profitable despite promising prospects. Inasmuch as we are likely to see more frequent reorganization and even more radical demands on people for changes in occupational behavior, it becomes necessary to delineate and differentiate the new kinds of roles which people are expected to perform on a continuing basis to facilitate the person-job fit.

These roles might be differentiated according to the career stage, the need levels, and the value systems they require, and the degree to which they relate to one or another of the personality dimensions—aggression, affection, dependency, ego ideal—I have outlined. If adaptation is the crucial element in organizational survival, as well in individual mastery, then these criteria for task differentiation should enhance adaptation for both.

Complementing the role differentiation, there must also be adequate structural definition in organizations which give particular attention to the distribution of power. Without adequate role power, a supervisor or manager at any level cannot provide adequate support and authority for those who report to him.

In the process of continuously reassessing tasks and roles within task requirements, it seems to me that it will be increasingly important to ask: What configuration of the variables I have outlined, and others which may be added, would characterize, define, and describe the persons most appropriate for the accomplishment of organizational tasks? That is, what career stage, what age- and stage-specific tasks, what value systems, what need level requirements, and what organizational adaptive tasks bring to the fore those feelings, thoughts, and behavior which are most relevant? There may even be thought given to what kind of tasks are most congenial to people in developmental crisis. For example, it might be most appropriate to assign a person who is not yet fully at mid-career, but who is between 38 and 40, experiencing the need to be his own man, who has a manipulative value system and stands at the self-actualization level in a company which is decentralizing, to aggressive managerial tasks requiring mobilization of a team of people to solve a critical marketing problem, which requires high risk and promises to pay off handsomely.

A broad educational effort should be undertaken so that people may better understand career issues, age issues, crisis issues, value issues, hierarchy of need issues, and organizational change requirements and can better engage with management in planning their own career and in continuously renegotiating their psychological contracts.

If people are to think more freely and more frequently about their occupational alternatives and career choices in keeping with changing configurations of needs, inevitably they will be involved in multiple career planning in anticipation of personal, professional, and organizational changes. For that planning to be effective and supported adequately by high level management, it will be necessary to have the upward appraisal system I suggested earlier in which subordinates appraise superiors on the degree to which they are helpful to them in their professional growth and development. Otherwise there will be little pressure on superiors to engage in such discussions. In addition, since all change involves the experience of loss and depressive feelings of varying intensity, it is necessary for organizations to evolve modes through which people can talk about their loss and change experiences so that the negative feelings which accompany them do not inhibit their adaptive efforts.

Supervisory Problems

The problems supervisors at any level deal with frequently are problems of individual feelings, thoughts, and behavior which create difficulties for the supervisor, for the supervisee, or for other employees. Often supervisors are baffled by the behavior and by the resistance of the supervisee to all of their efforts. Most do not begin to understand why such behavior comes about, let alone know what to do about it. The conceptions we have so far outlined can be particularly helpful in analyzing the behavior and determining a course of action.

A supervisor should always take time to write or talk through his own description of the problem at hand. After having summarized the issues as he sees them, including what he has said to the subordinate and the subordinate to him and what steps have so far been taken with what consequences, a number of helpful questions can be asked:

Where is the pain? That is, who is the most upset by this behavior? The supervisee? Peers? The supervisor? Others outside the organization? Usually the point of pain is the only point of leverage in a problem because people who experience no difficulty or pain are not about to be involved in attempting to change behavior, whether their own or somebody else's.

When did it begin? Problems which have a long history are unlikely to be changed by managerial activity. If, however, the supervisor can pinpoint the time when the behavior began, he can review what happened at that time and see in what way environmental forces may have been altered to precipitate the negative behavior. In such a case he may alter the environmental forces once more to restore the previous behavior.

What is happening to affection, aggression, dependency? That is, how are the drives and issues of dependency being managed? What is this person doing with his or her aggressions? What is he doing with the need to love and be loved? Is the aggression being directed to others? Is it being held in and dealt with by passive resistance? Does the person withdraw from others and no longer maintain friendships, or does he seek to aggrandize himself and boost his own self-image? And what is happening to his dependency needs? How is he handling them? Are the drives and dependency being handled in ways different than they were previously?

What is the nature of the ego ideal? That is, what does it take for this person to like himself? How is he trying to perceive himself? What aspirations does this person hold for him or herself and to what extent are they realizable in this organization or in this work?

Is this problem solvable? Not all problems are. Some merely remain as problems and simply have to be accepted as such.

If so, how? What steps can be taken to cope with the problems in light of the analysis being made?

Here is an example of a managerial problem as the manager who experienced it wrote it:

PRESENTATION

I work for a national organization with numerous divisions throughout the country. As regional manager, I oversee the work of several areas. My problem concerns Hal, an area head who reports to me.

Hal and I have worked for this organization for twenty-five years. He has always been a rather difficult person to work with, but our relationship and his performance have begun to decline further in recent months. I believe that this change coincides with a change in the organization. We have recently become much more centralized. The change was made by top management. Regional managers used to be responsible for so many widely scattered areas that, in effect, area heads ran their own shows with hardly any intervention from higher-ups. Presently, regional managers are responsible for fewer, smaller areas. Therefore, I have much more contact with Hal and supervise him closely.

Hal is an independent type and likes to have a free hand. He has always distrusted higher management and is active in a movement for middle management unionization. He seems to resent my closer supervision of him. The organization has moved toward participative management, and I believe in this and try to practice it. Hal tends to buck my efforts. In a meeting, for example, he tends to sit at the opposite end of the table from me and say very little. When a given topic has been covered and we're ten minutes beyond it, suddenly he volunteers his opinion on that topic.

He dislikes anything that threatens to alter his routine. When presented with a new way of doing things, he nods in agreement and then does everything just as he used to, working around the new system very adroitly. Recently I selected one of his subordinates to attend a management workshop without having had time to consult him beforehand. Hal made every effort to block the plan. He insisted first that this man could not be spared, and then that a different staff member be sent.

He has always been pretty isolated at work, with few friends. He has a special distaste for the telephone and prefers to handle matters through the mail. He likes to take his time and mull things over. He also is a stubborn character, all the more since the centralization.

I feel this problem could be solved somehow because it's an interpersonal one. I have discussed the situation with my superior. One idea we had was to have him work with computers, since his problems lie in the people area. However, he has long and useful experience as an area head, and I would not like to discard a competent manager if there is any way to ameliorate our working relationship.

Applying the mode of analysis outlined above, this problem might be studied as follows:

ANALYSIS

Where Is the Pain? Both men are in pain.

When Did It Begin? Although Hal has always had the personality described in the case, the situation has deteriorated since the new centralization.

Affection. Hal is described as "isolated." He seems to be holding back and trying to disavow needs for affection. Such a person may find it easier to get affection through a structured group like a union than through informal social relationships with coworkers.

Aggression. Hal expresses aggression passively. He evades and sabotages the wishes of his superiors not by direct attack, but by failing to cooperate. Getting involved with people inevitably presents the risk of conflict and anger. Hal apparently has structured his life to avoid this risk. He avoids having to give spontaneous responses by avoiding the telephone. Such behavior suggests that he keeps away from people so that he can contain his aggression.

Hal's aggression is stimulated by the change in the organization. Apparently, few people were involved in the decision to centralize. A change handed down from on high tends to anger most people, and it is particularly disturbing to those with personalities like Hal's. Centralization involves Hal with his superior and others. This forced human contact makes him angry. His safe, distant posture has been invaded, and he is fighting as if his home had been broken into. The problem of supervising the so-called independent worker often does not surface until a change in the organization makes closer contact necessary.

Dependency. Hal is described as "independent." But he isn't really. People like this try to deny their need for even healthy interdependency. If Hal were stable in his independence, he could accept interaction with others with equanimity. Some experiences in his life must have led him to feel that it is not safe to lean on anyone, particularly those in authority.

Ego Ideal. Hal's self-respect is interfered with by the new regime. It is important to him to feel that however small his operation is, he's in charge of it. With his energies significantly tied up in these emotional conflicts, he is not striving to a very high level of accomplishment.

Is It Solvable? Given the recent onset, there is hope for improvement.

How? Hal's personality won't change. But the regional manager can reduce Hal's feeling of being intruded upon by doing everything possible to bolster his self-image. He can seek out Hal's advice wherever possible and go to him first on many issues so that Hal will have advance knowledge about topics to be discussed in meetings. Then he can mull them over and have the chance to make helpful contributions in his own style.

OUTLINE FOR PROBLEM ANALYSIS

Where is the pain?
When did it begin?
What is happening to:
    Affection?
    Aggression?
    Dependency?
What is the nature of the ego ideal?
Is this problem solvable?
If so, how?

Chapter 4

Managing in the Future Tense

Organizations of the future will have to change more quickly and radically to cope with environmental changes. This means that they will have to be more decentralized and more flexible. At the same time, their employees will be increasingly better educated, with higher levels of aspiration and strong needs to demonstrate their competence and have an effect on their fates. Having attained relative affluence, they will also want to enjoy various aspects of life, including work life, more fully.

To be more decentralized and flexible and simultaneously to engage themselves with people who both want to act and are impelled to do so, organizations will have to give greater attention to leadership and to developmental activities which will enhance the capacity for flexible adaptation on the part of their employees. Inasmuch as leaders are the instruments of organizational cohesion, they are the pivots of organizational change. They are also the modes through which others relate to the organization, its purposes, goals, requirements, and obligations. It is out of identification with leadership that successive leadership develops and that developmental activities acquire significant meaning. These—leadership and development—must be supported by organizational structures, processes, and procedures that facilitate the most effective coping with the marketplace over the long term.

The more complex the environment is, the more complex and the more conceptual must be the models with which one works.

This is just as true for the psychology of motivation as it is for economics, marketing, finance, and control. This adaptation of psychoanalytic theory makes it possible to sustain an adaptive concept of organizational leadership through whatever changes may arise and to increase the adaptive skill and competence of employees whatever their level of education, experience, knowledge, and technical ability. That is, the mode of understanding people is sufficiently comprehensive and consistent in its basic frame of reference that it is unlikely to change its basic form, although it may become more highly refined with research and experience.

Managers must know and understand the psychology of motivation with the same degree of proficiency as they know marketing, manufacturing, economics, sales, engineering, and so on. Not every manager must be a master of all of these, but each must have a basic knowledge and understanding of people or he will be unable to meet the demands inside and outside of the organization that are inevitably to come. There are likely to be more and more controls from the bottom, whether formal or informal. There are likely to be greater concerns about organizational stress and its consequences for individual people, just as there is presently much concern about the impact of organizations on the physical environment. Given portable pensions and welfare protection, people are more likely to leave organizations when they are dissatisfied. People are less likely to be motivated by money alone and increasingly will want to relate to organizations as substitutes for the extended family. While younger people may deny this and avoid continuity in organizations, after a few years they must either find a place in an organization or go into business for themselves. Few can afford to do otherwise.

Inevitably, to become part of an organization is to become heavily dependent on the decisions of other people and on the fate of the organization. This in turn implies that people have a fundamental need to exert some control over the organization in order to have some control over their own fate. This pressure makes the leadership issue all the more important because either the organization will be abandoned to group process, and in the extreme to nonadaptive worker councils, as in some parts of Europe, or it will be compelled to be adaptive by appropriately aggressive leadership which has the capacity for interacting with followers toward ever more effective problem solving. We are witnessing a third alternative to these two extremes. On all sides there is increasing unionization of middle management, white collar, and professional people. Public employees have long been organized. Physicians have only recently started to organize. These are merely indicative of the growing move toward white-collar unionization. If the only way people can have an effect on their own fate is to become unionized, and unionization carries with it the risk of inhibiting innovation and adaptation, then there can be serious danger to the adaptation of all kinds of organizations. Change will be impossible except as a product of crisis and then will come about at considerable cost to individuals, organizations, and society as a whole. We have the alternative of adopting an adaptive leadership posture, of creating more effective means for the utilization of people as well as for changing organizations, or the leadership function will deteriorate into mere administration, something which has already happened with too many hospitals, school systems, universities, and civil service activities.

People who are abandoned by their leadership become enraged. People who organize to protect themselves, people who become unionized to protect themselves, usually do so out of desperation or distrust, knowing that they are likely to sacrifice individual merit and innovation for security. Often they do so, reluctantly. Only by that means have they been able to look out for themselves and make their influence felt.

The major barrier to the application of psychological insights to management is massive denial. By and large managers are reluctant to accept the validity of psychological forces. They are particularly reluctant to recognize the existence of unconscious motivation and primary process thinking. Most fear that to do so is to admit that they cannot be or are not in control of themselves, that there may be problems that they cannot resolve by themselves, that they may lose their motivation to achieve and compete if achievement and competition have irrational roots.

Some fear that too much psychological knowledge will inhibit their actions or undermine their authoritative functioning. Others want to have a world which can be neatly controlled by systems and numbers, where only the bottom line counts and human feelings can simply be excluded from consideration. Some feel helpless in the face of the complexity of human motivation. The same people who entertain complexity of finance, of engineering, of accounting, or even of the market-place seem to be intimidated to think of the complexity of motivation. Some of their fear is both natural and appropriate: unlike their preparation for these other functions, few have been taught to understand motivation well enough to feel comfortable in dealing with motivational conceptions. Some are fearful that such knowledge will enable them to harm others. While it is true that some people can be harmed if an untrained person seeks to be an amateur therapist, it is equally true that we are always operating with psychological assumptions of one kind or another. It is far wiser to know what kinds of assumptions one is working with and to be in a position to test these assumptions than to operate randomly and blindly. Managers cannot do much more damage to subordinates than they are already doing with anachronistic organizational structures with the crude methods of screening, assignment, appraisal, supervision, and compensation that are now being employed.

However, the directions I have outlined indicate that managers will no longer have the luxury of fear and therefore the freedom to freeze out issues of psychological motivation. More and more people will be pounding on their doors. More and more people will be demanding interaction with them. More and more will be insisting on their rights and privileges—in short upon continuous free negotiation of the psychological contract. Thus, managers will be compelled to interact with those who no longer bow or stand before them, but increasingly sit across the table from them.

Organizations are social instruments of people. People will use them to meet their own basic needs. The crucial sign of individual psychological health is the capacity to adapt to, to cope with, to master the environment and oneself, and to find gratification in living without exploiting others. Likewise, the fundamental criterion of organizational health is the capacity to adapt, to accomplish tasks, and to cope with the environment without having to destroy others or the environment in the process. As part of the process of protecting themselves people will increasingly lock themselves into organizations. Much as in some parts of Europe, companies are not free to discharge people either at blue-collar or white-collar levels, so increasingly such constraints will be pressed upon American corporations. This in turn means that executives will have to think more of how to make maximum use of personnel resources throughout working lifetimes. Thus, the emphases in this book on age and stage phases, crises, and proclivities are likely to become increasingly important. In addition, there will need to be more specific documentation of people's inability to perform given tasks before they may be laid off, transferred, demoted, or discharged as more and more such cases are taken to the courts, to regulatory agencies, and to arbitration. Just as companies are more rigidly circumscribed with respect to the effect of their manufacturing processes on the environment and their responsibilities to their host communities, so will they be more circumscribed about the psychological pollution they cause with respect to their employees. As there is further demonstration of the relationship between negative experiences at work and mental health, corporations will be compelled to take more positive steps to deal with those forces which create undue and unacceptable stresses for people in organizations. These include style of supervision, organizational structure, and organizational processes.

Thus, the contents of this book are not merely an effort to idealize the management profession and to make it into something other than management. Rather they are anticipating the trends and forces which management increasingly will face and providing guidance for coping effectively with them while maintaining the adaptive momentum of the organization.

References

Chapter 1

1. Michael A. Simpson, *American Medical News,* June 2, 1975.
2. Konrad Lorenz, *On Aggression* (New York, Bantam Books, 1967); also, Anthony Storr, *Human Aggression* (New York, Athenaeum, 1968).
3. Melanie Klein, "A Contribution to the Psychogenesis of Manic-Depressive States," in M. Klein, ed., *Contributions to Psychoanalysis, 1921-1945* (London, Hogarth, 1948).
4. Erik H. Erikson, *Childhood and Society,* 2d ed. (New York, Norton, 1963), chap. 7.
5. Robert W. White, "Ego and Reality in Psychoanalytic Theory," *Psychological Issues*, vol. III, no. 3 (New York, International Universities Press, 1963).

Chapter 2

6. Harry Levinson, *The Exceptional Executive* (Cambridge, Harvard University Press, 1968), chap. 2.
7. Harry Levinson, Charlton R. Price, Kenneth J. Munden, Harold J. Mandl, and Charles M. Solley, *Men, Management and Mental Health* (Cambridge, Harvard University Press, 1962).
8. Robert L. Kahn, Donald M. Wolfe, Robert P. Quinn, J. Diedrick Snoek, and Robert A. Rosenthal, *Organizational Stress* (New York, Wiley, 1964).
9. Laurence J. Peter and Raymond Hull, *The Peter Principle* (New York, Morrow, 1969).
10. Allan Mazur, "A Cross Species Comparison of Status in Small Established Groups," *American Sociological Review* 38:513-530 (October 1973).

References

11. Claude Desjardins, J. A. Maruniak, and F. H. Bronson, "Social Rank in House Mice: Differentiation Revealed by Ultraviolet Visualization of Urinary Marking Patterns," *Science* 182:4115, 939-941 (Nov. 30, 1973).
12. L. S. Ewing, "Fighting and Death from Stress in a Cockroach," *Science* 155:1035-36 (Feb. 24, 1967).
13. Arthur Kornhauser, *Mental Health of the Industrial Worker* (New York, Wiley, 1965).

Chapter 3

14. Robert Payne, *The Great Man* (New York, Coward-McCann & Geoghegan, Inc., 1974).
15. Harry Levinson et al., *Men, Management and Mental Health.*
16. Harry Levinson, *The Exceptional Executive,* chap. 2.
17. Harry Levinson et al., *Men, Management and Mental Health,* chaps. 9-11.
18. Harry Levinson, *Executive Stress* (New York, Harper & Row, 1972), chap. 12.
19. Richard C. Hodgson, Daniel J. Levinson, and Abraham Zaleznik, *The Executive Role Constellation* (Boston, Harvard Graduate School of Business Administration, 1965).
20. Paul R. Lawrence and Jay W. Lorsch, *Organization and Environment* (Boston, Harvard Graduate School of Business Administration, 1967).
21. Elliott Jaques, *Work, Creativity and Social Justice* (New York, International Universities Press, 1970); also Wilfred Brown, *The Earnings Conflict* (London, Heinemann, 1973).
22. Lawrence and Lorsch, *Organization and Environment.*
23. Jay W. Lorsch and John J. Morse, *Organizations and Their Members* (Cambridge, Harvard University Press, 1974).
24. Thomas H. Holmes and Richard H. Rahe, "Social Adjustment and Rating Scale," *Journal of Psychosomatic Research* 11:213 (1967); also Richard H. Rahe, Linda Bennett, Matti Siltanen, and Ranson J. Arthur, "Subjects' Recent Life Changes and Coronary Heart Disease in Finland," *American Journal of Psychiatry* 130:11, 1222-27 (November 1973).
25. Ralph G. Hirschowitz, "Crisis Theory: A Formulation," *Psychiatric Annals,* 3:33-49 (December 1973); also J. S. Tyhurst, "The Role of Transition States," *Symposium on Preventative and Social Psychiatry,* Walter Reed Army Medical Center (Washington, D.C., Government Printing Office, 1957).

26. Douglas H. Powell and Paul F. Driscoll, "Middle-Class Professionals Face Unemployment," *Transaction/Society* 10:18-26 (January 1973).

27. Harry Levinson, *The Great Jackass Fallacy* (Cambridge, Harvard University Press, 1973), chap. 10.

28. Harry Levinson, *The Exceptional Executive,* chap. 2.

29. Daniel J. Levinson, Charlotte M. Darrow, Edward B. Klein, Maria H. Levinson, and Braxton McKee, *The Psychosocial Development of Men in Early Adulthood and the Mid-Life Transition,* ed. D. F. Ricks, A. Thomas, and M. Roff, Life History Research and Psychopathology, vol. 3 (University of Minnesota Press, 1974).

30. Kenneth Keniston, *The Uncommitted* (New York, Dell, 1965).

31. Eli Goldston, "Executive Sabbaticals: About to Take Off?" *Harvard Business Review* 51:5, 57-68 (September-October 1973).

32. Harry Levinson, *Executive Stress,* chap. 24.

33. Samuel R. Connor and John S. Fielden, "R_x for Managerial Shelf Sitters," *Harvard Business Review* 51:6, 113-120 (November-December 1973).

34. Harry Levinson, *Emotional Health: In the World of Work* (New York, Harper & Row, 1964), chap. 18.

35. Harry Levinson, "Appraisal of *What* Performance?" *Harvard Business Review* 54:30-46, 160 (July-August 1976).

36. Elliott Jaques, *Equitable Payment*, 2d ed. (Carbondale and Edwardsville, Southern Illinois University Press, 1970).

37. Levinson Reciprocation Scale, Cambridge, The Levinson Institute, 1975.

38. Gordon W. Allport, P. E. Vernon, and Gardner Lindzey, *A Study of Values* (Boston, Houghton Mifflin, 1960).

39. Charles L. Hughes and Vincent S. Flowers, "Shaping Personnel Strategies to Disparate Value Systems," *Personnel* 50:8-23 (March-April 1973); also Clare Graves, "Levels of Existence: An Open System Theory of Values," *Journal of Humanistic Psychology* 10:2, 131-155 (Fall 1970).

40. Abraham H. Maslow, *Personality and Motivation* (New York, Harper & Row, 1954).

41. J. F. Veiga, "The Mobile Manager at Mid-Career," *Harvard Business Review* 51:115-119 (January-February 1973).

42. Jaques, *Work, Creativity and Social Justice*, chap. 3.

43. Daniel J. Levinson *et al., Psychological Development of Men.*

44. David Gutman, "The Hunger of Old Men," *Transaction* 9:53-66 (November-December 1971).